CW01560651

CHIN

TRAVEL GUIDE

2025-2026

From Dynasties to Skyscrapers: Your Go-To Travel
Guide for Chinese Culture, History & Adventure

Jack Clover

Copyright © 2025 Jack Clover

All rights reserved. No part of this publication may be reproduced, distributed, or transmitted in any form or by any means, including photocopying, recording, or other electronic or mechanical methods, without the prior written permission of the author, except in the case of brief quotations used in reviews and certain other non-commercial uses as permitted by copyright law.

Table of Content

SCAN HERE TO VIEW THE MAP OF

CHINA

My Journey Through China: A Personal Experience

China isn't just a place you visit—it's a country that **pulls you in, overwhelms you, and leaves you changed**. When I first set foot in Beijing, I thought I knew what to expect: grand temples, chaotic streets, and a culture that stretched back thousands of years. But what I experienced was something **far more immersive, far more alive** than I ever imagined.

I remember my first morning in Beijing, stepping out into the crisp air near the Forbidden City. The scent of freshly steamed baozi from a nearby stall mixed with the faint aroma of incense from a hidden temple courtyard. Locals zipped past on e-bikes, a blend of tradition and modernity in motion. I grabbed a Jianbing (a crispy, savory pancake wrapped in egg, scallions, and hoisin sauce) from a street vendor. That first bite? **A perfect introduction to China's love affair with food.**

Shanghai took my breath away in a different way. Walking along The Bund at night, I felt like I had stepped into the future—neon lights bouncing off the water, high-speed trains humming in the distance. But just a short ferry ride away in the old town of Zhujiajiao, I was transported back in time, drifting along canals as if I were in a Chinese watercolor painting.

Then there was **Guilin**, where I climbed up Xianggong Hill at dawn. As the mist lifted over the Li River, revealing those surreal, karst mountains, I realized something—China isn't just about the places you see. It's about the **feeling** of standing somewhere that has seen centuries of history, the quiet moments in a tea house, the laughter shared with strangers who become friends over a hot pot meal.

China is vast, dynamic, and full of surprises. And as I explored, I learned one key lesson: **it's not a country you simply check off a list—it's a place that stays with you long after you've left.**

Chapter 1: China's Must-See Destinations & Hidden Gems

China is a country of **mind-blowing contrasts**—from ultra-modern cities to untouched rural landscapes, from ancient relics to futuristic skyscrapers. This chapter takes you through **the absolute must-visit destinations** that define China's cultural and historical essence, while also revealing **lesser-known gems** that most tourists miss.

Iconic Destinations You Can't Skip

- **Beijing:** Walk through history at the **Forbidden City (4 Jingshan Front St, Dongcheng, Beijing, 100009)** and climb the **Great Wall (Badaling section: Yanqing District, Beijing, 102112).**
- **Shanghai:** Experience the skyline at **The Bund (Zhongshan East 1st Rd, Huangpu District, Shanghai, 200002)** and get lost in the old-world charm of **Yu Garden (218 Anren St, Huangpu, Shanghai, 200010).**
- **Xi'an:** Stand face-to-face with the **Terracotta Army (Lintong District, Xi'an, Shaanxi, 710612)** and cycle the **Ancient City Wall** for breathtaking views.
- **Guilin & Yangshuo:** Drift down the **Li River**, surrounded by **dreamlike karst mountains** straight out of a painting.
- **Chengdu:** Get up close with **giant pandas** at the **Chengdu Research Base (1375 Panda Ave, Chenghua, Chengdu, 610081)** and indulge in **authentic Sichuan hot pot.**

Hidden Gems Worth Exploring

- **Zhangjiajie:** The inspiration for *Avatar's* floating mountains—hike through **Zhangjiajie National Forest Park (Wulingyuan District, Zhangjiajie, Hunan, 427400)** for jaw-dropping scenery.

- **Zhujiajiao Water Town:** Just outside Shanghai, this **ancient canal town** feels like stepping back in time.
- **Kanas Lake, Xinjiang:** A pristine alpine paradise in China's far northwest—stunning **turquoise waters surrounded by snowy peaks**.
- **Dongchuan Red Land, Yunnan:** Often called "China's Red Carpet," this **vibrant, Mars-like landscape** is a dream for photographers.

This chapter **sets the stage for your adventure**—whether you're drawn to the **grandeur of the Great Wall** or the **serenity of a hidden village**, you'll find something here that speaks to your traveler's soul.

Top Cities & Iconic Landmarks

China is a country where **ancient history meets cutting-edge modernity**, and its cities reflect this dynamic energy. Whether you're after **cultural treasures, futuristic skylines, or breathtaking natural wonders**, these cities and their **iconic landmarks** are must-sees on any journey through China.

---

1. Beijing – The Heart of China's History

📍 **Why Visit?** Beijing is where **imperial China meets the modern world**. As the country's capital, it's packed with historic landmarks, cultural relics, and **authentic Chinese experiences**.

* **The Forbidden City** (4 Jingshan Front St, Dongcheng, Beijing, 100009) – A **massive palace complex** that once housed emperors for centuries. Walk through its grand courtyards and intricate halls.
* **The Great Wall of China** (Badaling: Yanqing District, Beijing, 102112) – No trip to China is complete without hiking this **legendary structure**, which stretches over 13,000 miles.
* **Temple of Heaven** (1 Tiantan E Rd, Dongcheng, Beijing, 100061) – A masterpiece of **Ming dynasty architecture** where emperors once prayed for good harvests.
* **Summer Palace** (19 Xinjiangongmen Rd, Haidian District, Beijing, 100091) – A serene escape with **pavilions, gardens, and Kunming Lake**, perfect for a relaxing afternoon.

---

2. Shanghai – The Future Meets the Past

 Why Visit? China's **economic powerhouse** is a thrilling mix of **futuristic skyscrapers** and **historical charm**.

* **The Bund** (Zhongshan East 1st Rd, Huangpu, Shanghai, 200002) – Walk along this iconic waterfront for **skyline views of the Huangpu River**.
* **Yu Garden & Bazaar** (218 Anren St, Huangpu,

Shanghai, 200010) – A **classical Chinese garden** surrounded by markets selling traditional snacks and souvenirs.

❖ **Shanghai Tower** (501 Yincheng Middle Rd, Lujiazui, Pudong, Shanghai, 200120) – China's **tallest building** with **360-degree views** from its observation deck.

❖ **Tianzifang** – A maze of **narrow alleys filled with cafes, artisan shops, and creative boutiques**—perfect for exploring Shanghai's artsy side.

---

3. Xi'an – China's Ancient Capital

📍 **Why Visit?** Home to the legendary **Terracotta Warriors**, Xi'an is one of China's **most historic cities**.

❖ **Terracotta Army** (Lintong District, Xi'an, Shaanxi, 710612) – A breathtaking sight of **8,000 life-sized warriors**, each with unique facial features, guarding Emperor Qin's tomb.

❖ **Xi'an City Wall** – One of the **best-preserved ancient city walls** in China, offering stunning views of the city.

❖ **Muslim Quarter** – A **vibrant food street** packed with local specialties like **lamb skewers and roujiamo (Chinese burgers)**.

---

* **Best Time to Visit:** September to December, when the fields are at their most colorful.
* **Top Experience:** Watching the sunrise over **Luoxiagou (Sunset Valley)**, as the land transforms into a surreal painting.

---

2. Wulingyuan Scenic Area – Zhangjiajie's Lesser-Known Twin

📍 **Location:** Hunan Province
✦ **Why Go?** While Zhangjiajie is famous for its **Avatar-like floating mountains**, Wulingyuan offers a **similar landscape without the crowds**. This **UNESCO-listed site** is full of towering sandstone pillars, deep canyons, and misty forests.

* **Hidden Gem: Bailong Elevator**—a **glass elevator built into a cliff** that offers jaw-dropping views.
* **Best Hike: Golden Whip Stream**, a peaceful walk surrounded by towering peaks and lush bamboo forests.

---

3. Danxia Landform – China's "Rainbow Mountains"

📍 **Location:** Zhangye, Gansu Province
✦ **Why Go?** These **striking, multicolored rock**

formations look like something out of a **fantasy world**, with layered hues of red, yellow, and orange stretching for miles.

• **Best Time to Visit:** Late afternoon, when the sunlight enhances the mountain's vibrant colors.
  • **Must-See Spot: Binggou Danxia Scenic Area**, a quieter, equally stunning section of the park.

---

4. Guizhou's Miao & Dong Villages – A Cultural Escape

📍 **Location:** Guizhou Province
✦ **Why Go?** For a deep dive into **China's minority cultures**, the **Miao and Dong ethnic villages** in Guizhou offer an **authentic glimpse** into traditional lifestyles.

• **Must-Visit Village: Xijiang Qianhu Miao Village**, the **largest Miao village in China**, with wooden stilt houses and daily cultural performances.
  • **Hidden Gem: Zhaoxing Dong Village**, home to **beautiful drum towers and covered bridges**, surrounded by rice terraces.

---

5. Yading Nature Reserve – "The Last Shangri-La"

Location: Sichuan Province
Why Go? If you love **pristine alpine scenery**, Yading is **one of the most breathtaking places in China**, with snow-capped peaks, turquoise lakes, and untouched forests.

- **Must-See Spot: Milk Lake**, a stunning blue-green glacial lake with a backdrop of towering mountains.
- **Best Time to Visit: Autumn**, when the landscape is painted in golden hues.

---

6. Kanas Lake – China's Secret Switzerland

Location: Xinjiang Uygur Autonomous Region
Why Go? Hidden in the **Altai Mountains**, Kanas Lake is a **stunning glacial lake** with **crystal-clear waters, pine forests, and Kazakh yurts** scattered along the grasslands.

- **Top Activity:** Take a **boat ride on Kanas Lake** for panoramic views of the snow-covered mountains.
- **Hidden Gem:** Visit **Hemu Village**, a remote, fairytale-like settlement where nomadic Kazakh people live.

---

7. Shaxi Ancient Town – A Forgotten Tea Horse Road Stop

Location: Yunnan Province
Why Go? If you want to experience **China's old-world charm without the commercialized crowds**, Shaxi is a **peaceful, well-preserved ancient town** that once thrived along the **Tea Horse Road**.

• **Must-Do:** Wander through **Sideng Square**, a historic market surrounded by traditional wooden buildings.
• **Local Tip:** Stay in a **centuries-old guesthouse** and enjoy the slow pace of village life.

---

8. Ejina Desert Poplar Forest – A Golden Wonderland

Location: Inner Mongolia
Why Go? Every autumn, this desert transforms into a **golden sea of poplar trees**, creating one of **China's most surreal landscapes**.

• **Best Time to Visit:** Late September to mid-October, when the trees are at their peak color.
• **Hidden Gem:** Visit **Heicheng Ruins**, a **mystical ancient city buried in the desert**.

---

9. Tongli Water Town – A Hidden Venice

📍 **Location:** Jiangsu Province (Near Suzhou)
✨ **Why Go?** While many water towns near Shanghai are packed with tourists, Tongli remains **peaceful and authentic**, with **ancient stone bridges, wooden boats, and canals lined with red lanterns**.

* **Must-See Spot: Retreat & Reflection Garden,** a **UNESCO-listed classical Chinese garden.**
* **Best Experience: Glide through the town on a wooden boat ride** at sunset.

---

10. Hulunbuir Grasslands – China's Wild Frontier

📍 **Location:** Inner Mongolia
✨ **Why Go?** If you dream of **vast open landscapes, rolling green fields, and nomadic culture**, the **Hulunbuir Grasslands** are a must-visit.

* **Must-Do:** Stay in a **traditional Mongolian yurt** and experience **horseback riding across endless grasslands.**
* **Best Time to Visit: Summer**, when the grasslands are lush and full of wildflowers.

China is full of **hidden wonders**, each offering a **different side of the country's beauty, history, and culture**. Whether you're trekking through **rainbow mountains, exploring forgotten villages, or cruising along serene waterways**, these off-the-beaten-path destinations promise **authentic adventures away from the crowds**.

🚀 **Next up:** How to travel wisely in China—saving money, avoiding scams, and making the most of your journey!

UNESCO World Heritage Sites

China boasts a **staggering 56 UNESCO World Heritage Sites**, making it one of the world's top countries for cultural and natural heritage. From **ancient wonders** to **breathtaking landscapes**, these sites showcase **China's deep history, architectural marvels, and stunning**

biodiversity. Here are some of the **most iconic and unmissable** ones:

---

1. The Great Wall of China – A Monument of Endurance

📍 **Location:** Stretches across northern China
✦ **Why Go?** One of the most **legendary landmarks in the world**, the Great Wall winds through mountains, valleys, and deserts, standing as a testament to **China's history and resilience.**

- **Best Sections to Visit:**

  - **Mutianyu** – Less crowded, well-preserved, and scenic.
  - **Jinshanling** – Best for hiking with dramatic views.
  - **Jiankou** – Wild, rugged, and untouched for adventurous travelers.

- **Insider Tip:** Visit **at sunrise or sunset** for fewer crowds and stunning scenery.

---

2. Forbidden City – The Heart of Imperial China

📍 **Location:** Beijing
✦ **Why Go?** Once home to **24 emperors**, this **lavish**

palace complex is a masterpiece of traditional Chinese architecture, featuring **900+ buildings adorned with golden roofs and intricate carvings**.

• **Must-See Highlights:**

- **Hall of Supreme Harmony** – The most important structure.
- **Palace of Tranquil Longevity** – Hidden beauty away from the crowds.
- **The Imperial Garden** – A peaceful retreat within the grand palace.

• **Pro Tip:** Buy tickets online in advance—entry is limited daily!

---

3. Terracotta Army – An Underground Marvel

 Location: Xi'an, Shaanxi Province
 Why Go? Discovered in 1974, this **army of 8,000+ life-sized warriors**, each with unique facial expressions, was built to **guard Emperor Qin Shi Huang in the afterlife**.

• **Best Way to Explore:**

- **Pit 1** – The largest and most impressive.
- **Pit 2 & 3** – Showcases generals and archers with more intricate details.

- **Emperor's Tomb** – Still unexcavated but believed to hold unimaginable treasures.

◆ **Local Tip:** Combine your visit with **Xi'an's Muslim Quarter** for amazing street food!

---

4. Mogao Caves – The Library of Ancient China

📍 **Location:** Dunhuang, Gansu Province
✦ **Why Go?** These **Buddhist cave temples**, decorated with over **45,000 square meters of murals**, are a **treasure trove of Silk Road history and art**.

◆ **Must-See Caves:**

- **Cave 96** – Features a stunning **35-meter-tall Buddha statue**.
- **Cave 17** – Known as the **"Library Cave"**, containing ancient manuscripts.

◆ **Pro Tip:** Access to certain caves is limited—**book a guided tour** for the best experience.

---

5. Mount Huangshan – China's Most Beautiful Mountain

📍 **Location:** Anhui Province

✨ **Why Go?** Famous for its **otherworldly granite peaks, twisted pine trees, and floating seas of clouds**, Mount Huangshan has inspired poets and artists for centuries.

- **Best Views:**

  - **Bright Summit Peak** – Best for sunrise views.
  - **Flying-Over Rock** – A famous balanced rock formation.
  - **West Sea Canyon** – A breathtaking hiking route with dramatic scenery.

- **Local Tip:** Take the **cable car up and hike down** to fully enjoy the experience.

---

6. Classical Gardens of Suzhou – Living Works of Art

📍 **Location:** Suzhou, Jiangsu Province

✨ **Why Go?** These **meticulously designed Chinese gardens** are perfect for experiencing **traditional landscape art**, with **pavilions, ponds, and rock formations** creating a tranquil atmosphere.

- **Top Gardens to Visit:**

  - **Humble Administrator's Garden** – The largest and most famous.

Chapter 2: The Cultural & Historical Depth of China

China's culture is **one of the oldest and most influential in the world**, spanning over **5,000 years of dynasties, traditions, and philosophies**. From the **ancient Silk Road to the rise of modern metropolises**, this chapter delves into **China's fascinating cultural evolution**, key historical moments, and how its deep-rooted traditions continue to shape daily life today.

Key Highlights in This Chapter:

■ **The Rise and Fall of China's Great Dynasties** – Discover how dynasties like the Tang, Song, Ming, and Qing shaped the country.

■ **Philosophy & Spirituality** – Learn about Confucianism, Daoism, and Buddhism and their lasting influence on Chinese society.

■ **China's Role in Global Trade** – Explore the impact of the Silk Road and maritime trade on world history.

■ **Art, Literature & Calligraphy** – A look into China's most treasured artistic traditions.

■ **Festivals & Traditions** – Understand the significance of Lunar New Year, the Mid-Autumn Festival, and other cultural celebrations.

■ **Modern China & Cultural Preservation** – How China balances rapid modernization with its centuries-old heritage.

This chapter gives you a **deeper appreciation** of China beyond its landmarks—**it's about the soul of the nation**, from its ancient wisdom to the dynamic society it is today.

A Brief History of China

China's history is a **5,000-year saga of dynasties, revolutions, and cultural evolution**, making it one of the most **enduring civilizations** on Earth. From the legendary Xia Dynasty to today's global influence, **China's story is one of resilience, innovation, and transformation**.

Ancient Beginnings (c. 2100 BCE – 221 BCE)

The origins of Chinese civilization trace back to the **Xia Dynasty (c. 2100 BCE – 1600 BCE)**—believed to be China's first ruling dynasty, though evidence remains scarce. The

Shang Dynasty (1600 BCE – 1046 BCE) introduced **bronze casting, oracle bone writing, and early forms of governance.** This era was followed by the **Zhou Dynasty (1046 BCE – 256 BCE)**, which introduced the **Mandate of Heaven**, a concept that justified rulers' divine right to rule. Confucianism and Daoism also emerged during this time, shaping Chinese thought for centuries.

Imperial China & the Great Dynasties (221 BCE – 1912 CE)

- **Qin Dynasty (221 BCE – 206 BCE)** – China was unified for the first time under **Qin Shi Huang**, who standardized currency, weights, and writing. He also began the construction of the **Great Wall of China**.
- **Han Dynasty (206 BCE – 220 CE)** – Often called China's **Golden Age**, this period saw the expansion of the Silk Road, advances in science, and the promotion of Confucianism.
- **Tang & Song Dynasties (618 CE – 1279 CE)** – China became a global economic and cultural superpower, pioneering **gunpowder, paper money, and printing technology**.
- **Yuan Dynasty (1279 CE – 1368 CE)** – The Mongols, led by **Kublai Khan**, ruled China, integrating it into a vast Eurasian empire.
- **Ming Dynasty (1368 CE – 1644 CE)** – Famous for **the Forbidden City, naval expeditions by Zheng He, and the Great Wall's expansion**.
- **Qing Dynasty (1644 CE – 1912 CE)** – The last imperial dynasty, known for cultural refinement but

also foreign invasions and internal strife, eventually leading to its collapse.

Revolution, War & Modern China (1912 CE – Present)

The **fall of the Qing Dynasty in 1912** led to the establishment of the **Republic of China** under Sun Yat-sen. However, political instability and warlordism plagued the nation.

- **Chinese Civil War (1927 – 1949)** – A brutal conflict between the Nationalists (Kuomintang) and the Communists, ending with the Communist victory in 1949.
- **People's Republic of China (1949 – Present)** – Founded by **Mao Zedong**, the country went through drastic social and economic changes, including the **Great Leap Forward** and the **Cultural Revolution**.
- **Economic Rise (1980s – Today)** – Since the **economic reforms of Deng Xiaoping**, China has rapidly industrialized, becoming the world's **second-largest economy** while still preserving its deep cultural heritage.

China Today

Now, China is a **global powerhouse**, seamlessly blending **ancient traditions with cutting-edge innovation**. Its **history is visible everywhere**, from the preserved **hutongs of Beijing** to the **high-speed trains connecting**

megacities. Understanding China's past is the **key to appreciating its present and future**.

The Balance of Tradition & Innovation

China is a nation where **thousands of years of tradition** coexist with **cutting-edge modernity**. From ancient Confucian values shaping social norms to futuristic AI-driven cities, China has mastered the **art of preserving its heritage while leading global innovation**.

Tradition in Everyday Life

Despite rapid urbanization and technological advancements, **Chinese traditions remain deeply rooted in society:**

■ **Family Values & Filial Piety** – Confucian principles still guide family structures, emphasizing respect for elders and strong kinship ties.

■ **Festivals & Ancestral Worship** – Events like **Chinese New Year, Qingming Festival, and the Mid-Autumn Festival** continue to be widely celebrated.

■ **Traditional Medicine & Wellness** – **Traditional Chinese Medicine (TCM)**, including acupuncture and herbal remedies, remains a respected form of healthcare.

■ **Arts & Handicrafts** – Calligraphy, porcelain making, and tea culture thrive, often blended with modern aesthetics.

Innovation & Modernization

China is at the forefront of **technological advancements and economic growth**, balancing the old with the new:

🚀 **Smart Cities & AI Integration** – Cities like **Shenzhen and Shanghai** lead in AI, fintech, and 5G infrastructure.

🚀 **High-Speed Rail Network** – China has the world's largest bullet train system, seamlessly connecting ancient towns with futuristic megacities.

🚀 **E-commerce & Digital Payment** – Cash is nearly obsolete, with **WeChat Pay and Alipay** dominating transactions—even at street markets.

🚀 **Space Exploration & Green Energy** – China is investing heavily in **space missions, electric vehicles, and renewable energy**, making sustainability a priority.

Where Tradition Meets Innovation

China's genius lies in how it **integrates old and new** rather than replacing one with the other:

◆ **Ancient Temples in Modern Skylines** – In cities like **Beijing and Hangzhou**, you'll find historic temples standing alongside futuristic skyscrapers.

◆ **Tech-Driven Preservation** – The Forbidden City uses AI and digital modeling to restore and maintain its ancient architecture.

◆ **Cultural Influence in Global Trends** – From Chinese streetwear brands embracing traditional embroidery to pop culture reviving classical poetry, the past and present blend seamlessly.

China's ability to **preserve its heritage while embracing the future** is what makes it so **dynamic and** fascinating—a country where **centuries-old traditions continue to thrive in an ultra-modern world**.

Key Cultural Customs & Etiquette

China's rich cultural heritage extends beyond its landmarks—it's embedded in **everyday interactions, traditions, and social etiquette**. Whether you're visiting a temple, dining with locals, or navigating business meetings, understanding **Chinese customs** will help you **connect more deeply with the culture and avoid unintentional missteps**.

🖐 Greetings & Social Etiquette

■ **Handshakes Over Hugs** – A handshake is the most common greeting, often accompanied by a slight nod. **Hugging and cheek kissing are rare**, especially with strangers.

■ **Addressing People Formally** – Use **titles and surnames** (e.g., "Wang Laoshi" for Teacher Wang or "Li Jingli" for Manager Li) rather than first names.

■ **Modesty & Humility** – Compliments are often deflected rather than directly accepted—it's a sign of humility rather than rudeness.

🍜 Dining Etiquette

■ **Chopstick Rules** – Never stick chopsticks upright in rice (it resembles incense offerings for the dead). Avoid pointing chopsticks at others.

■ **Serving Others First** – It's polite to pour tea or serve food to others before yourself. If someone fills your cup, tap the table with two fingers as a sign of gratitude.

■ **Bargaining at Markets** – Haggling is expected at local markets, but always remain polite and friendly.

🏠 Visiting Homes & Temples

■ **Gift-Giving Matters** – If invited to a home, bring a small gift like tea, fruit, or alcohol, but avoid clocks (which symbolize death). Gifts are often refused once or twice before being accepted.

■ **Shoes Off Indoors** – In many homes and some temples, it's customary to remove shoes before entering.

■ **Respecting Sacred Spaces** – When visiting temples, dress modestly, avoid loud conversations, and never turn your back to a statue of Buddha.

🥟 Business & Professional Etiquette

■ **Exchanging Business Cards** – Use both hands to give and receive cards, and take a moment to read the card before putting it away.

■ **Indirect Communication** – The Chinese often value diplomacy over direct confrontation. **"Yes" doesn't always mean agreement**—sometimes, it's a polite way to acknowledge what was said.

■ **Face (Mianzi) Matters** – Public embarrassment or confrontation is avoided at all costs. Maintaining "face" (respect and reputation) is crucial in business and social interactions.

■ **Plan regional routes** for **efficient travel** and minimal transit time.

🐷 Budgeting & Cost-Saving Tips

China offers a **range of experiences** for every budget. This section includes:
■ **Daily expense estimates** (budget, mid-range, luxury).
■ **Saving money on transport, accommodation, and attractions.**
■ **Where to get the best local meals without overspending.**

🏛 Transportation: Getting Around China

China's vast transportation network can be **intimidating but efficient**. Learn about:
■ **High-speed trains vs. domestic flights** – which is better for your route?
■ **Metro & bus systems** – navigating cities like a local.
■ **Apps like WeChat, Alipay, and Didi** – making payments and booking rides seamlessly.

This chapter **equips you with all the practical knowledge needed** to plan a **stress-free, exciting, and budget-friendly trip**—whether you're exploring bustling cities, ancient villages, or breathtaking landscapes.

Best Time to Visit China

China's sheer size means its **climate varies significantly** from region to region. The best time to visit depends on **your destinations, weather preferences, and the type of experiences you want.**

✿ **Spring (March–May) – Ideal for Sightseeing & Nature**

◼ **Mild temperatures (10–25°C/50–77°F)** – Comfortable for outdoor exploration.
◼ **Cherry blossoms & lush landscapes** – Especially beautiful in **Beijing, Shanghai, and Hangzhou.**
◼ **Fewer tourists than summer** – But avoid **Qingming Festival (April),** when locals travel heavily.

Best for: Hiking the **Great Wall,** exploring **Jiuzhaigou Valley,** and visiting **Suzhou's classical gardens.**

☀ Summer (June–August) – Hot, Humid & Peak Tourist Season

■ **Warm to extremely hot (25–40°C/77–104°F)** – Especially in **Beijing, Shanghai, and inland cities**.
■ **Best time for Tibet & mountainous regions** – Places like **Yunnan, Sichuan, and Xinjiang** are more accessible.
■ **School holidays mean bigger crowds & higher prices** – Attractions can be packed, especially in July & August.

Best for: Exploring **Tibet, Zhangjiajie National Forest Park**, and escaping to **Qingdao's beaches**.

✿ Autumn (September–November) – The Absolute Best Season

■ **Perfect weather (15–25°C/59–77°F)** – Clear skies, cool temperatures, and low humidity.
■ **Golden landscapes & fall foliage** – Stunning in **Jiuzhaigou, the Great Wall, and the Yellow Mountains**.
■ **Fewer crowds compared to summer** – But **avoid Golden Week (October 1–7)** when millions of locals travel.

Best for: Visiting **historical sites, hiking, and experiencing China's natural beauty**.

❄ **Winter (December–February) – Cold, But Unique Experiences**

■ **Snow-covered landscapes** – Harbin's **Ice & Snow Festival** is a must-see.
■ **Best for budget travelers** – Hotels & flights are cheaper outside Chinese New Year.
■ **Chilly, but fewer tourists** – Perfect for a quieter, more authentic experience in cities like **Beijing & Xi'an.**
✖ **Harsh cold in northern China** – Beijing, Harbin, and Inner Mongolia can reach **-20°C (-4°F).**

Best for: Skiing in China's northeast, seeing frozen waterfalls, and enjoying hotpot in Chengdu.

⏳ When to Avoid Traveling

⃠ **Chinese New Year (Late January–Mid-February)** – Cities empty as locals return home, but transport is packed.
⃠ **Golden Week (October 1–7)** – One of the busiest travel times, with high prices and crowded attractions.
⃠ **Labour Day Holiday (May 1–3)** – Another short but busy travel period.

📌 Final Verdict: The Best Months to Visit

✔ **March–May & September–November** – Ideal for mild weather, fewer crowds, and beautiful scenery.

✔ **June–August** – Great for visiting high-altitude regions like Tibet but avoid crowded tourist hotspots.

✔ **December–February** – Best for winter activities, cultural festivals, and budget-friendly travel.

Choosing **the right season** ensures you get the best out of China, whether you're looking for **adventure, history, food, or relaxation.**

Visa & Entry Requirements

Traveling to China requires **advance planning**, especially when it comes to visas and entry requirements. China has **strict visa regulations,** and not preparing properly could lead to delays or denied entry. This section will help you **navigate the visa process smoothly** so you can focus on your adventure.

■ Do You Need a Visa for China?

Most travelers **need a visa** to enter China, except for a few exceptions:

■ **Visa-Free Transit (72/144 hours)** – If you're stopping in cities like **Beijing, Shanghai, or Guangzhou** en route to another country, you may qualify for a **visa-free transit** stay of **72 or 144 hours**.

■ **Hong Kong & Macau** – Many nationalities can visit **visa-free** for **7 to 90 days** (depending on nationality).

However, visiting mainland China requires a separate visa.

■ **Special Administrative Regions** – Travelers visiting **Hainan Island** can enter **visa-free for up to 30 days** under certain conditions.

■ Tourist Visa (L-Visa) – The Most Common Option

The **Tourist Visa (L-Visa)** is required for most visitors and allows stays of **30, 60, or 90 days**, depending on the application.

📌 **How to Apply for a China Tourist Visa**

[1] **Check your eligibility** – Most nationalities must apply before arriving.

[2] **Prepare required documents:**

- Passport **valid for at least 6 months** with at least **one blank page**.
- **Completed visa application form** (available online).
- **Recent passport-sized photo** (must meet Chinese visa photo standards).
- **Proof of itinerary** – Flight reservations, accommodation bookings, and a travel itinerary.
- **Invitation letter (if applicable)** – Required if visiting family or friends.

  [3] **Submit application at a Chinese embassy/consulate** or through an authorized visa

center.

4 **Pay the visa fee** – Costs vary by nationality (typically **\$30–\$140 USD**).

5 **Wait for approval** – Processing time is usually **4–7 business days** (or faster with an express service).

Entry Process: What to Expect at Immigration

Upon arrival, you'll go through **immigration and customs**. Here's what to expect:

■ **Fingerprint scans & photo verification** – A standard security measure.

■ **Health declaration (if required)** – Occasionally needed during public health concerns.

■ **Visa check & passport stamp** – Keep a copy of your **entry stamp** for reference.

🔦 **Tip:** Have your first night's hotel address and a return/onward ticket ready, as immigration officers may ask for proof of stay.

Visa Extensions & Multi-Entry Visas

If you plan to stay longer, you can apply for a **visa extension** at a local **Public Security Bureau (PSB) office** in China. Multi-entry visas are available for frequent travelers and **business visitors**.

🪔 Important Travel Restrictions & Rules

🚫 **No entry for damaged passports** – Make sure your passport is in good condition.

🚫 **Strict rules on political materials** – Avoid carrying anything critical of the Chinese government.

🚫 **VPNs & Internet restrictions** – Many websites (Google, WhatsApp, Instagram) are blocked. Download a **VPN before arrival** if needed.

📌 Final Visa & Entry Tips

✔ **Apply for your visa at least 1 month before your trip** to avoid delays.

✔ **Check for updated policies** as rules can change.

✔ **Have printed copies of your hotel bookings & itinerary** to avoid entry issues.

✔ **If using visa-free transit, ensure your itinerary qualifies** to prevent being denied entry.

Following these steps ensures a **smooth arrival** so you can **enjoy your trip hassle-free!**

Budgeting for China

China offers **a wide range of travel experiences**, from **budget backpacking** to **luxury stays**. Whether you're looking for a **cost-effective adventure** or a **high-end cultural escape**, careful budgeting can help you **maximize your trip without overspending**. Here's a breakdown of what to expect in terms of **costs, spending tips, and money-saving hacks**.

💰 Average Daily Travel Costs in China

Your daily budget will depend on **your travel style**:

Expense Category	Budget Traveler ($)	Mid-Range ($)	Luxury ($)
Accommodation	$10–$30 (hostels, budget hotels)	$40–$100 (3-4 star hotels)	$150+ (5-star hotels, luxury stays)
Food	$5–$15 (street food, local restaurants)	$20–$50 (sit-down restaurants)	$80+ (fine dining, private dining experiences)

Transport	$1–$5 (public transport, shared bikes)	$10–$30 (high-speed train, taxis)	$50+ (private drivers, business-class flights)
Attractions	$5–$20 (museums, temples)	$30–$60 (guided tours, national parks)	$100+ (VIP tours, private experiences)
Total Daily Budget	$25–$50	$80–$200	$300+

🏠 Accommodation Costs & Money-Saving Tips

- **Budget: Hostels & budget hotels** start at **$10–$30 per night**. Look for **capsule hotels** for an affordable yet comfortable stay.
- **Mid-Range:** Comfortable **3–4 star hotels** cost **$40–$100 per night**. Staying slightly **outside city centers** can save you money.
- **Luxury:** High-end hotels like **The Peninsula Beijing** or **Aman Summer Palace** cost **$150+ per night**, with top-tier amenities.

💡 **Money-Saving Tip:** Use **Ctrip (Trip.com) or Agoda** for hotel discounts, and check for deals on **WeChat mini-programs**.

🍜 Food Costs & How to Eat Cheaply

- **Street food & local restaurants:** Meals like **dumplings, noodles, and fried rice** cost **$1–$5** per dish.
- **Mid-range dining:** A nice **local restaurant** costs **$10–$20 per person**.
- **Fine dining:** Expect to pay **$50–$150 per meal** at high-end restaurants.

💡 **Money-Saving Tip:** Eat where **locals eat**—small noodle shops, hole-in-the-wall dumpling stalls, and **food courts** in malls offer great meals at **low prices**.

🛗 Transportation Costs & Budget-Friendly Options

- **Metro & buses:** Super cheap at **$0.30–$1 per ride**. Metro cards help you save even more.
- **High-speed trains:** A **second-class ticket** from **Beijing to Shanghai** costs around **$75**, while first-class is about **$120**.

- **Taxis & Didi (China's Uber):** Short rides start at **$2–$5,** but avoid taxis at **airports & tourist areas** as they tend to overcharge.
- **Domestic flights:** Can range from **$50–$200,** but high-speed trains are often cheaper and more convenient.

💡 **Money-Saving Tip:** Use the **12306 China Railway app** for train tickets and **Didi** instead of taxis for cheaper rides.

📖 Attractions & Entrance Fees

- **Budget-friendly sites:** Many **parks, temples, and museums** charge **$5–$20**.
- **Popular attractions:** Tickets to **the Great Wall, Forbidden City, and Terracotta Army** range from **$20–$40**.
- **Luxury experiences:** Private guides or special access tours cost **$100+** per person.

💡 **Money-Saving Tip: Visit attractions early** to avoid peak-hour price hikes, and use **student or senior discounts** if eligible.

🛍 Shopping & Souvenirs – How to Avoid Overpaying

- **Street markets & bargain shops** offer silk, tea, jade, and souvenirs at **$5–$50.**
- **Luxury malls & designer brands** are on par with international prices.
- **Haggle at markets** – Expect to bargain down by **30–50%** at places like **Beijing's Silk Market or Shanghai's Yuyuan Bazaar.**

💡 **Money-Saving Tip:** Use **Alipay or WeChat Pay** for discounts and cashback offers at certain shops.

📱 Payment Methods – How to Handle Money in China

- **Mobile Payments Dominate:** Most locals use **Alipay or WeChat Pay** instead of cash or credit cards.
- **Foreign Credit Cards:** Only accepted at major hotels, airports, and some big stores.
- **Cash:** Still needed in smaller towns or local markets.

💡 **Money-Saving Tip:** Exchange money **before arrival** or at **Bank of China ATMs** for the best rates.

📌 Final Budgeting Tips for China

✔ **Use public transport instead of taxis** to save money.
✔ **Book trains & flights in advance** to get the best prices.
✔ **Eat like a local** at street food stalls and food courts.
✔ **Haggle at markets** to avoid paying inflated tourist prices.
✔ **Get a SIM card or eSIM** to access mobile payment apps.

With careful budgeting, **China can be an affordable destination** without sacrificing incredible experiences. Whether you're traveling on a **backpacker budget or a luxury plan**, smart spending ensures **a stress-free, enjoyable trip!**

Packing Essentials & Travel Insurance

Packing for China requires **a strategic approach**—from handling different **climates** to ensuring you have **the right travel documents**. Whether you're exploring the **bustling streets of Shanghai**, trekking the **mountains of Zhangjiajie**, or experiencing **rural villages**, having the right gear **makes all the difference**.

🎒 Packing Essentials – What You Must Bring

1 Travel Documents & Money Essentials

✔ **Passport & Visa:** Always carry **a digital and physical copy** of your passport and visa.

✔ **Travel Insurance Details:** Keep a **printed copy** and digital version of your policy.

✔ **Cash & Cards:** Bring some **Chinese Yuan (CNY)** for small transactions. **Alipay & WeChat Pay** are widely used, so set them up beforehand.

✔ **International Credit/Debit Card:** China's ATMs accept **Visa and Mastercard** at major banks, but not everywhere.

💡 **Tip:** Always keep a **separate stash of emergency cash** in case mobile payments or cards don't work.

---

2 Clothing & Footwear – Dressing for China's Climate

China's climate varies greatly, so pack according to the **season & region**:

✔ **Spring & Autumn (March–May, Sept–Nov):** Lightweight clothing, a light **jacket**, and **comfortable shoes**.

✔ **Summer (June–August): Breathable clothes, sunscreen, sunglasses**, and a **hat** for heat protection. **Mosquito repellent** is a must for humid areas.

✔ **Winter (Dec–Feb):** Northern China is **freezing**, so pack **thermal layers, a heavy coat, gloves, and a scarf.** Southern China is milder but can be **damp and chilly**.

💡 **Tip:** If visiting temples or rural villages, **modest clothing** is recommended.

---

3 Tech & Gadgets – Staying Connected in China

✔ **Unlocked Phone & VPN: A must-have** since many Western sites (**Google, WhatsApp, Instagram**) are blocked. Download a **VPN** before arriving.
✔ **Portable Charger & Power Adapter:** China uses **Type A, C, and I plugs** (220V).
✔ **Translation Apps: Google Translate** (with offline mode) or **Pleco** (a great Chinese dictionary).
✔ **Navigation Apps: Baidu Maps** (for local accuracy) & **Metro apps** for subway routes.

💡 **Tip:** Download **WeChat**—it's the go-to app for **communication, payments, and local info**.

---

4 Health & Hygiene Must-Haves

✔ **Medications & First Aid Kit:** Carry prescription meds with a **doctor's note** and common over-the-counter drugs like **painkillers, motion sickness tablets, and antihistamines**.
✔ **Hand Sanitizer & Wet Wipes:** Public restrooms often **lack soap or paper towels**.

✔ **Tissues & Toilet Paper:** Always have some, as public toilets **rarely provide them**.

💡 **Tip:** Pharmacies in China stock **local medicine brands**, but finding **Western brands** can be difficult.

🛡 Travel Insurance – Why You Need It in China

Unexpected situations **can happen**, and **good travel insurance** protects against:

✔ Medical Emergencies & Hospitalization

- Healthcare in major cities like **Beijing & Shanghai** is high-quality but **expensive**.
- In rural areas, **facilities may lack English-speaking staff**—insurance helps cover **evacuations to better hospitals**.

✔ Lost Luggage & Stolen Belongings

- If your bag goes missing on a **high-speed train** or flight, insurance **covers replacement costs**.
- **Pickpocketing isn't common** in China, but **markets & crowded areas** can be targets.

✔ Trip Cancellations & Delays

- **China's unpredictable weather** (typhoons, heavy snowfall) can cause **flight/train cancellations**.

- **Pandemic-related travel restrictions** can lead to last-minute itinerary changes.

Tip: Choose **a policy that covers adventure sports** if you plan to **hike, ski, or cycle** in remote areas.

📌 Final Packing & Insurance Tips

✔ **Check China's latest travel requirements** for **visa, vaccinations, and entry rules**.
✔ **Pack light but smart**—laundry services are **affordable** in hotels.
✔ **Choose comprehensive travel insurance** to cover **medical, theft, and cancellations**.
✔ **Download essential apps before arrival** for easy navigation & communication.

Being **well-prepared** ensures **a hassle-free adventure**, letting you focus on **exploring China's rich landscapes & culture** without unnecessary stress! 🚀

Chapter 4: Festivals & Cultural Celebrations

China's festivals are a **spectacle of color, tradition, and deep-rooted cultural significance.** From the grand fireworks of **Chinese New Year** to the mesmerizing **lantern-lit sky** of the **Mid-Autumn Festival**, these celebrations provide **a window into the soul of Chinese culture.** Whether you're joining in on **dragon boat races,**

witnessing **Buddhist rituals,** or enjoying **street parades,** China's festivals offer an unforgettable experience.

This chapter covers **the major festivals, their significance, and how travelers can best experience them,** including **where to go, what to expect,** and **how to participate like a local.** You'll also find **tips on timing your visit to coincide with these events** and **how to navigate the crowds during peak festival seasons.**

Chinese New Year & Lantern Festival

China's **biggest and most important festival, Chinese New Year** (春节, *Chūnjié*), marks the start of the **lunar calendar** and is a time of **family reunions, feasting, and fireworks.** It is followed by the **Lantern Festival** (元宵节, *Yuánxiāo Jié*), a dazzling display of **lanterns, performances, and moonlit festivities** that officially concludes the **New Year celebrations.**

🎊 Chinese New Year (Spring Festival) – The Biggest Celebration in China

📅 **When?** January/February (First day of the Lunar New Year)

📍 **Best Places to Experience:** Beijing, Shanghai, Guangzhou, Hong Kong, Harbin

Chinese New Year is a nationwide event that shuts down entire cities as millions travel home to be with their families. Known as the **largest human migration on Earth**, this period is both **exciting and chaotic** for travelers.

⬩ **What to Expect During Chinese New Year**

✔ **Fireworks & Firecrackers:** The sky **explodes with fireworks** at midnight, believed to scare away evil spirits.
✔ **Red Everywhere: Red lanterns, banners, and envelopes (*hóngbāo*)** symbolize **luck and prosperity**.
✔ **Feasting on Traditional Dishes:** Families gather for a **lavish reunion dinner**, featuring dumplings (*jiǎozi*), fish (*symbolizing abundance*), and spring rolls.
✔ **Dragon & Lion Dances:** Performed in **temples and streets**, these dances **ward off bad luck** and welcome prosperity.
✔ **Temple Fairs:** Markets filled with **folk performances, craft stalls, and street food**—great for soaking up the festive energy.

📍 **Traveler Tip: Cities can be extremely crowded**, with **transportation at peak capacity.** Book accommodations **months in advance** and avoid traveling **right before or after the holiday.**

📍 Lantern Festival – A Magical End to the New Year Celebrations

■ **When?** 15th day of the Lunar New Year (late January–February)

📍 **Best Places to Experience:** Pingxi (Taiwan), Xi'an, Nanjing, Beijing

The **Lantern Festival** is the **grand finale of the New Year celebrations,** where **thousands of glowing lanterns** light up the night sky in a breathtaking display of **hope and renewal.**

- ◆ **How the Lantern Festival is Celebrated**

✔ **Releasing Sky Lanterns:** People write **wishes for the future** on lanterns before releasing them into the sky.

✔ **Lantern Displays & Parades:** Cities host **elaborate lantern exhibitions,** some shaped like **dragons, animals, and historical figures.**

✔ **Solving Lantern Riddles:** Lanterns often have **riddles attached,** and solving them brings **good fortune.**

✔ **Eating Glutinous Rice Balls (*Tangyuan*):** These **sweet, round dumplings** symbolize **family unity and togetherness.**

✔ **Lion & Dragon Dances:** The **final performances** of the season, adding excitement and rhythm to the night.

💡 **Traveler Tip: Pingxi, Taiwan,** is famous for its **Sky Lantern Festival,** where **thousands of lanterns** float into the sky at once—**a truly magical sight!**

Why You Should Experience These Festivals

✔ **Unmatched cultural immersion** – Witness China's **rich traditions** in full display.

✔ **A chance to celebrate with locals** – Join in the excitement of **fireworks, feasting, and festivities.**

✔ **Spectacular photo opportunities** – From **lantern-lit skies** to **dragon dances**, these events are **visual masterpieces.**

If you're planning a trip to China, **timing it around Chinese New Year and the Lantern Festival** will give you a **once-in-a-lifetime experience** of **joy, tradition, and spectacular celebrations!** 🚀

Dragon Boat Festival & Mid-Autumn Festival

China's **Dragon Boat Festival** and **Mid-Autumn Festival** are two of the country's most cherished cultural celebrations, both deeply rooted in history and filled with vibrant traditions. From the **thrill of dragon boat races** to the **sweetness of mooncakes under a full moon**, these festivals offer travelers a **glimpse into China's rich folklore and communal spirit.**

🛶 Dragon Boat Festival (端午节, Duānwǔ Jié) – A Celebration of Speed & Remembrance

■ **When?** Fifth day of the fifth lunar month (May/June)

📍 **Best Places to Experience:** Hong Kong, Guangzhou, Hangzhou, Suzhou, Beijing

The **Dragon Boat Festival** is a high-energy event honoring **Qu Yuan**, a patriotic poet from the Warring States period. The festival is famous for its **fast-paced dragon boat races**, where synchronized paddlers power **colorful, dragon-shaped boats** through the water.

⬧ **How the Dragon Boat Festival is Celebrated**

✔ **Dragon Boat Races:** Teams compete in **fierce, adrenaline-pumping races** in rivers and lakes across China.

✔ **Eating Sticky Rice Dumplings (*Zongzi*):** These **leaf-wrapped rice dumplings** are stuffed with **savory or sweet fillings** and symbolize **protection and remembrance**.

✔ **Wearing Herbal Pouches:** Locals wear **fragrant sachets filled with medicinal herbs** to **ward off evil spirits and disease**.

✔ **Balancing Eggs:** A fun tradition where **people try to stand an egg upright** at noon—believed to bring good luck.

✔ **Hanging Mugwort & Calamus:** Homes are decorated with **these plants** to **repel insects and bad luck**.

📍 **Traveler Tip: Hong Kong's Stanley Dragon Boat Festival** is one of the most exciting places to witness the races, with **thousands of spectators and a carnival-like atmosphere**.

⬤ Mid-Autumn Festival (中秋节, **Zhōngqiū Jié**) – Mooncakes & Family Reunions

📅 **When?** 15th day of the eighth lunar month (September/October)
📍 **Best Places to Experience:** Beijing, Shanghai, Guangzhou, Xi'an, Hong Kong

The **Mid-Autumn Festival** is a time for **family reunions, moonlit gatherings, and storytelling**. It celebrates the **full moon**, symbolizing **harmony and togetherness**.

- ◆ **How the Mid-Autumn Festival is Celebrated**

✔ **Eating Mooncakes:** The **star treat of the festival,** these rich pastries are filled with **lotus seed paste, red bean, or salted egg yolk.**
✔ **Lantern Displays & Moon Gazing:** Parks and riverbanks light up with **stunning lanterns**, while families gather to **admire the full moon.**
✔ **Worshipping the Moon Goddess, Chang'e:** According to legend, **Chang'e, the Moon Goddess**, lives on the moon, and people **make offerings to her for blessings.**
✔ **Dragon & Lion Dances:** Some regions host **dazzling performances**, adding to the festive spirit.
✔ **Fire Dragon Dance (Hong Kong):** In Hong Kong's Tai

Hang neighborhood, a **gigantic dragon covered in incense sticks** dances through the streets—an incredible sight!

💡 **Traveler Tip:** If you want a **breathtaking Mid-Autumn experience**, head to **Hangzhou's West Lake** or **Victoria Harbour in Hong Kong**, where **lanterns float on the water** under the full moon.

Why You Should Experience These Festivals

✔ **Witness breathtaking traditions** – From **dragon boat races** to **fire dragon dances**, these festivals showcase **China's cultural heritage** at its best.
✔ **Taste festival-exclusive delicacies** – Enjoy **sticky rice dumplings during the Dragon Boat Festival** and **delicious mooncakes in autumn**.
✔ **Join in the festive atmosphere** – Whether you're **cheering at a boat race** or **gazing at lantern-lit skies**, these events create **unforgettable memories**.

By experiencing the **Dragon Boat Festival and Mid-Autumn Festival**, you'll gain **a deeper appreciation of China's traditions, folklore, and sense of community**. 🚀

Lesser-Known Local Festivals

While major festivals like **Chinese New Year** and the **Mid-Autumn Festival** steal the spotlight, China is also home to **countless regional and ethnic celebrations** that offer travelers an **authentic, off-the-beaten-path cultural experience.** These **lesser-known festivals** are where you'll find **fascinating traditions, unique rituals, and warm local hospitality**—perfect for travelers seeking something different!

🔥 Torch Festival (火把节, Huǒbǎ Jié) – A Fiery Spectacle of the Yi People

📓 **When?** Sixth lunar month (July/August)
📍 **Best Places to Experience:** Yunnan, Sichuan, and Guizhou provinces

The **Torch Festival** is one of the most visually stunning celebrations in China, particularly among the **Yi, Bai, and Naxi ethnic groups**. It is a festival of **fire, dance, and tribal pride**, symbolizing the **defeat of evil spirits** and a **wish for a bountiful harvest.**

• **How It's Celebrated**

✔ **Torch-Lit Parades:** Thousands of people march through villages holding **flaming torches**, illuminating the night sky.

✓ **Bonfire Dances:** Locals **dance in circles around towering bonfires,** singing folk songs and playing traditional instruments.

✓ **Bullfighting & Wrestling Competitions:** A thrilling part of the festival, showcasing **strength and courage.**

✓ **Fireworks & Dragon Dances:** Some regions include **dragon and lion dances,** as well as **firework displays.**

💡 **Traveler Tip:** Head to **Xichang, Sichuan,** where the **Torch Festival lasts for three days** and includes **fireworks, wrestling, and a torch parade through the city.**

🐂 Sisters' Meal Festival (姐妹饭节, Jiěmèi Fàn Jié) – The Miao People's Valentine's Day

🕊 **When?** Third lunar month (April)

📍 **Best Places to Experience:** Guizhou province, especially Taijiang County

Known as the **"oldest Valentine's Day in China,"** the **Sisters' Meal Festival** is a **romantic and colorful event** celebrated by the **Miao ethnic group.** It is a time for **young women to express their love through food and traditional attire.**

✦ **How It's Celebrated**

✔ **Sisters' Rice Exchange:** Young women prepare **dyed sticky rice** wrapped in leaves and secretly place it in pouches for suitors.

✔ **Hidden Messages in Food:** The number of **chopsticks or other items** hidden in the rice sends a **coded message**—two chopsticks mean **love is reciprocated**, while one means **better luck next time!**

✔ **Silver & Embroidery Fashion Show:** Miao women wear **stunning silver headdresses and intricate embroidered dresses** during grand parades.

✔ **Horse Racing & Bullfighting:** These events **add excitement** to the celebrations.

📍 **Traveler Tip:** If you want to experience an **ancient, romantic festival filled with folk music and colorful dress, this is a must-see!**

💦 Water-Splashing Festival (泼水节, Pōshuǐ Jié) – A Joyful Wet & Wild Celebration

📅 **When?** April 13–15
📍 **Best Places to Experience:** Xishuangbanna, Yunnan Province

Celebrated by the **Dai ethnic minority**, the **Water-Splashing Festival** marks the **Dai New Year** and is one of China's **most playful and interactive festivals.** Expect **three days of water fights, dragon boat races, and temple rituals!**

* **How It's Celebrated**

✔ **Massive Water Battles:** Locals and visitors **drench each other with buckets, hoses, and water guns**—it's believed to **wash away bad luck** for the new year.
 ✔ **Lantern Floating & Dragon Boat Races:** In the evenings, people **release lanterns on the river** and enjoy **lively boat races**.
 ✔ **Dai-Style Barbecues & Performances:** The streets are filled with **grilled fish, tropical fruit, and cultural performances**.
 ✔ **Temple Visits & Blessings:** The festival starts with **Buddhist prayers and rituals** at local temples.

 Traveler Tip: Be prepared to get **soaked!** Dress in **quick-dry clothing** and **store electronics in waterproof bags**.

Lusheng Festival (芦笙节, Lúshēng Jié) – The Grandest Miao Music Festival

 When? Varies (September–November)
 Best Places to Experience: Guizhou Province

The **Lusheng Festival** is **a mesmerizing music and dance festival** celebrated by the **Miao ethnic minority**. It is named after the **Lusheng,** a traditional bamboo wind instrument.

* **How It's Celebrated**

✔ **Lusheng Music & Dance Performances:** Miao men play the **lusheng** while women perform **beautifully choreographed dances** in traditional dress.
✔ **Buffalo Fighting & Horse Racing:** These **competitive events** add excitement to the festival.
✔ **Massive Parades & Costume Displays:** Miao women wear **stunning silver headdresses** and embroidered clothing for **grand processions**.
✔ **Community Feasting:** Expect **delicious ethnic dishes** shared among locals and guests.

💡 **Traveler Tip:** If you love **music, dance, and cultural immersion**, this festival is a **must-see in rural China**.

Why You Should Experience These Festivals

✔ **Authentic, off-the-beaten-path cultural experiences** – These festivals take place in **less-touristy regions**, offering a **more immersive experience.**

✔ **Vibrant traditions & unique celebrations** – From **fire parades** to **musical gatherings,** these festivals let you see a **different side of China.**

✔ **Incredible photo opportunities** – Whether it's the **glow of torches, colorful rice offerings,** or **giant water battles,** these festivals are **visually stunning.**

By **venturing beyond the well-known holidays,** you'll **discover hidden cultural gems** and experience the **soul of China's diverse ethnic traditions.** 🚀

Chapter 5: How to Navigate & Communicate in China

China is a **massive, fast-paced country** with an extensive transport system and a language that can feel overwhelming for first-time visitors. But don't worry—navigating and communicating in China is **easier than you might think** once you know a few key tips!

This chapter will **equip you with essential travel skills**, covering everything from **how to get around efficiently** to **overcoming language barriers**. Whether you're **hopping on high-speed trains, catching a taxi without speaking Mandarin**, or **using translation apps**, this guide will ensure you **explore China confidently and stress-free**.

◆ What You'll Learn in This Chapter

■ **Mastering Public Transport** – How to use **trains, metros, buses, and taxis** like a local.

■ **Essential Mandarin Phrases** – Key words and phrases to help you **order food, ask for directions, and communicate in daily situations**.

■ **Navigating Without Mandarin** – Smart travel hacks, **translation apps, and useful gestures** to help you get by.

■ **Understanding Chinese Addressing System** – How to **read signs, find locations, and give directions to drivers**.

■ **Mobile Payments & Travel Apps** – The **best apps for maps, taxis, and cashless payments** to make your trip smooth.

By the end of this chapter, you'll be **confident in exploring China independently**, no matter where you go!
■ ■ 🗣

Public Transport & High-Speed Trains

China's public transport system is **one of the most advanced and efficient in the world**. Whether you're zipping between cities on a **high-speed train**, hopping on a **metro** in major urban hubs, or taking a **bus** to reach off-the-beaten-path destinations, getting around China is **affordable, convenient, and often faster than flying**.

◢ **High-Speed Trains (Gaotie, 高铁)**

China's **high-speed rail network** is the **largest in the world**, connecting almost every major city. It's often the **best way to travel between cities** due to its speed, comfort, and affordability.

■ **Speeds:** Trains can reach **350 km/h (217 mph)**, making a trip from **Beijing to Shanghai (~1,200 km)** take only **4.5 hours.**
■ **Booking Tickets:** You can book tickets **online via Trip.com, 12306.cn (China's official site), or travel**

agencies. Buy early, as trains fill up fast!

■ **Classes: 2nd Class (budget-friendly), 1st Class (more space), and Business Class (luxury seats).**

■ **Stations:** Train stations are **huge and busy**, so arrive at least **45 minutes early** for security checks and boarding.

■ **Luggage:** There's no strict baggage limit, but try to pack light for easy movement.

● Metro Systems in Major Cities

China's **biggest cities**—Beijing, Shanghai, Guangzhou, Shenzhen, Chengdu, and Xi'an—have **ultra-modern, efficient subway systems**.

■ **Affordable:** Fares usually range between **¥2-¥10 ($0.30-$1.50 USD)** depending on distance.

■ **English-Friendly:** Metro stations have **English signage**, and ticket machines usually offer **English language options**.

■ **Payment Options:** Use a **metro card**, buy single-use tickets, or pay with **Alipay/WeChat Pay** in some cities.

■ **Peak Hours:** Avoid **7-9 AM** and **5-7 PM** when metros are extremely crowded.

■ Buses & Long-Distance Coaches

For budget travelers and those venturing into **rural areas**, buses and long-distance coaches can be a great option.

■ **City Buses:** Inexpensive (~¥1-¥3), but **require exact change or metro cards**. Some cities allow **WeChat/Alipay payments**.

■ **Long-Distance Buses:** Useful for reaching **smaller towns and remote locations** not connected by trains. Tickets can be purchased at **bus stations or online**.

■ **Sleeper Buses:** For overnight trips, sleeper buses have **reclining seats or small beds**, but they can be **cramped and less comfortable** than trains.

🚕 Taxis & Ride-Sharing (DiDi)

Taxis are widely available, but **many drivers don't speak English**.

■ **Apps Like DiDi (China's Uber):** Use **DiDi Chuxing** (download before arrival) for an easier ride-hailing experience.

■ **Fares & Payments:** Most taxis are **metered**, but some drivers may prefer cash. DiDi allows **card & digital wallet payments**.

■ **Tip for Non-Mandarin Speakers:** Have your **destination written in Chinese characters** or use **Google Translate** to show the driver.

🚲 Biking & Walking

China is **bike-friendly**, with shared bike services like **Meituan Bike & HelloBike** in major cities. Simply scan a QR code to rent a bike! 🚲

Walking is also **a great way to explore**, especially in places like **Shanghai's Bund, Beijing's hutongs, and ancient towns like Lijiang**.

Final Tips for Navigating China

■ **Use WeChat or Alipay** for metro, bus, and ride-hailing payments.

■ **Download Baidu Maps or Amap (Gaode Maps)**—Google Maps is **not always accurate** in China.

■ **Always carry your passport**—it's required for train travel and some metro ticket purchases.

Master these transport tips, and you'll be **moving around China like a local in no time!** 🚩

Taxis, Ride-Sharing & Biking

Getting around China's bustling cities and scenic countryside is **easier than ever** thanks to a **wide range of transport options**. Whether you need a **quick taxi ride**, a **convenient ride-share**, or want to **explore on two wheels**, there's a **transport solution for every traveler**.

🚕 Taxis: What You Need to Know

Taxis are **widely available** in cities and towns across China, but there are a few things to keep in mind:

■ Fares & Pricing

- Most taxis start at **¥10-¥14 ($1.50-$2 USD)** for the first **3 km (1.8 miles)**, with **¥2-¥3 ($0.30-$0.45 USD) per additional km**.
- In smaller towns, fares are **cheaper**, while major cities like Beijing and Shanghai may have **higher base fares**.
- **Late-night rides (after 11 PM)** may have a **surcharge** of up to 30%.

■ How to Get a Taxi

- **Street Hailing**: In major cities, just wave at a taxi with a **green light on the dashboard**—it means it's available.
- **Taxi Stands**: Found at **airports, train stations, and shopping malls**—often the best place to grab a reliable taxi.
- **Hotel Concierge**: If language is a barrier, ask your hotel to **call a taxi for you**.
- **Use an App**: DiDi (滴滴) is China's version of Uber—more on that below!

▓ Avoiding Taxi Scams

- **Always use metered taxis**—avoid drivers who refuse to use the meter.
- **Have your destination written in Chinese characters** (Google Translate can help).
- **Beware of "black taxis"** (unlicensed drivers who overcharge tourists).

🚗 Ride-Sharing with DiDi (滴滴出行)

DiDi is **China's Uber**, and it's the **most convenient way to book a ride** if you don't speak Mandarin.

▓ Why Use DiDi?

- No need to **flag down taxis**—just book from your phone.
- **Set your destination in English**, and the app translates it for the driver.
- **Pay directly in the app** using **WeChat Pay, Alipay, or a foreign credit card** (in some cities).
- **Safer than street taxis**—all rides are tracked in the app.

▓ How to Use DiDi

1. **Download the app** (DiDi Chuxing) before arriving in China.

2. **Select your ride type** (DiDi Express = cheapest, DiDi Premier = premium service).
3. **Input your destination** and confirm pickup.
4. **Check the license plate and driver's name** before entering the car.

◆ *Tip:* If your **DiDi app is in Chinese**, switch to "DiDi Global" for English support.

🚲 Biking: The Best Way to Explore Like a Local

China's cities have **embraced bike-sharing**, making it an **easy, fun, and eco-friendly way to explore.**

▓ Top Bike-Sharing Services
🚲 **Meituan Bike (**美团单车**)** – Yellow bikes, easy to rent with **WeChat Pay or Alipay.**
🚲 **HelloBike (**哈啰单车**)** – Best for **longer rides**, requires **ID verification** for use.
🚲 **Alipay Mini Program Bikes** – Rent directly **inside the Alipay app**—super convenient!

▓ How to Rent a Shared Bike

1. **Open the app** (WeChat, Alipay, or Meituan).
2. **Scan the QR code** on the bike.
3. **Start riding!**
4. **Park in designated areas** and lock the bike to end the ride.

■ Where to Ride

🚲 **Beijing's Hutongs** – Cycle through charming old alleyways.

🚲 **Shanghai's French Concession** – A scenic ride under tree-lined streets.

🚲 **Xiamen's Island Ring Road** – Coastal views with a dedicated bike lane.

🚲 **Hangzhou's West Lake** – A peaceful, iconic cycling route.

Final Tips for Taxis, Ride-Sharing & Biking

■ **Always carry cash or have WeChat Pay/Alipay ready**—some taxis don't accept foreign cards.

■ **Use DiDi for a stress-free experience**—it's the easiest option if you don't speak Mandarin.

■ **Bike-sharing is great for short distances**—just make sure to park legally.

With **taxis, DiDi, and bike-sharing, getting around China is easier than ever**—just pick the option that fits your adventure best! 🏯🚲

Essential Mandarin Phrases & Apps

China's rapid modernization means that in major cities, you'll find **some English signage and speakers**, but don't expect it everywhere. **Knowing a few key Mandarin**

phrases (or having the right apps) can make your trip **smoother and more enjoyable.**

📌 Essential Mandarin Phrases for Travelers

Even if you don't plan on speaking full sentences, **these survival phrases** will help in common situations:

✋ Basic Greetings & Politeness

- **Hello** – 你好 (*nǐ hǎo*)
- **Thank you** – 谢谢 (*xièxiè*)
- **You're welcome** – 不客气 (*bú kè qì*)
- **Excuse me / Sorry** – 对不起 (*duì bù qǐ*)
- **Goodbye** – 再见 (*zài jiàn*)

🚕 Getting Around

- **Where is...?** – ...在哪里? (*...zài nǎ lǐ?*)
- **I want to go to...** – 我要去... (*wǒ yào qù...*)
- **How much is the fare?** – 车费多少钱? (*chē fèi duō shǎo qián?*)
- **Stop here, please** – 请在这里停 (*qǐng zài zhè lǐ tíng*)
- **Is there a subway station nearby?** – 附近有地铁站吗? (*fù jìn yǒu dì tiě zhàn ma?*)

🍽 Ordering Food & Drinks

- **I want this one** – 我要这个 (*wǒ yào zhè gè*)

- **No spice, please** – 不要辣 (*bú yào là*)
- **Do you have vegetarian options?** – 有素食吗? (*yǒu sù shí ma?*)
- **Check, please** – 买单 (*mǎi dān*)

🛍 Shopping & Bargaining

- **How much is this?** – 这个多少钱? (*zhè gè duō shǎo qián?*)
- **It's too expensive!** – 太贵了! (*tài guì le!*)
- **Can you give me a discount?** – 可以便宜一点吗? (*kě yǐ pián yí yī diǎn ma?*)

🧰 Emergencies & Help

- **Help!** – 救命! (*jiù mìng!*)
- **Call the police!** – 报警! (*bào jǐng!*)
- **I'm lost** – 我迷路了 (*wǒ mí lù le*)
- **I need a doctor** – 我需要医生 (*wǒ xū yào yī shēng*)

◆ *Tip:* **Tone is important in Mandarin**, so if you're struggling, using a **translation app** can be a lifesaver!

📱 Must-Have Apps for Navigating China

China's digital ecosystem is **different from the West**, and **Google services won't work** without a VPN. Here are the **apps you'll need** for a smooth trip:

🗺 Navigation

📍 **Baidu Maps (**百度地图**)** – The best **Chinese alternative to Google Maps**. More accurate than Apple Maps in China.
📍 **Amap (**高德地图**)** – Another **highly detailed map app** used by locals.

📑 Translation

📍 **Pleco** – The **best Chinese-English dictionary**, with offline support and handwriting recognition.
📍 **Google Translate (with VPN)** - If you have a **VPN**, it's great for translating signs, menus, and conversations.
📍 **iTranslate** – A good alternative for real-time translation.

🚍 Transport & Ride-Hailing

📍 **DiDi (**滴滴**)** – The **Uber of China**, essential for booking rides without needing to talk to drivers.
📍 **12306 (**铁路**12306)** – The official app for **booking train tickets** in China.

💴 Payments & Currency Exchange

📍 **WeChat (**微信**)** – Used for **everything**, from chatting to **paying for food, transport, and shopping**.
📍 **Alipay (**支付宝**)** – Another **super useful** payment app—many places only accept WeChat Pay or Alipay.

🍽️ Food & Dining

📌 **Meituan (**美团**)** – Best for **ordering takeout and finding restaurants** with local reviews.
📌 **Dianping (**大众点评**)** – China's version of Yelp, perfect for checking **restaurant ratings and recommendations**.

🛍️ Shopping & Deals

📌 **Taobao (**淘宝**)** – China's **Amazon equivalent**, great for shopping.
📌 **JD.com (**京东**)** – Another **popular online shopping platform**.

🚀 Final Tips for Communication & Apps in China

⬛ **Download all essential apps before your trip**—some require phone number verification.
⬛ **Consider a Chinese SIM card or pocket Wi-Fi** for reliable internet access.
⬛ **If you can't speak Mandarin, use a translation app**—locals appreciate the effort!

Mastering **a few key phrases** and **using the right apps** will make your **China trip much easier and more enjoyable!** 🙂●

Chapter 6: Food & Culinary Experiences Across China

China's cuisine is as vast and diverse as its landscapes, with **each region offering distinct flavors, techniques, and specialties**. From the fiery spices of Sichuan to the delicate dim sum of Cantonese cuisine, **food is an essential part of the Chinese travel experience**.

In this chapter, we'll dive into:
 ✔ **The Eight Great Cuisines of China** – A breakdown of the country's most famous regional culinary traditions.
 ✔ **Must-Try Dishes** – Iconic foods like **Peking duck, xiaolongbao (soup dumplings), and Lanzhou hand-pulled noodles**.

✔ **Street Food & Night Markets** – The best places to sample authentic, affordable Chinese food.

✔ **Tea Culture & Traditional Beverages** – Exploring China's world-renowned tea culture, plus other drinks like baijiu (Chinese liquor).

✔ **Dining Etiquette & Ordering Tips** – Essential table manners and how to order like a local.

✔ **Foodie Destinations** – The top cities for culinary adventures, from **Chengdu for hotpot** to **Guangzhou for dim sum**.

Whether you're a street food lover or a fine dining enthusiast, this chapter will help you **navigate China's rich culinary scene with confidence and curiosity.** 🍜

Regional Cuisine Breakdown

China's culinary landscape is incredibly diverse, shaped by geography, climate, and cultural influences. The **Eight Great Cuisines of China (**八大菜系**, Bā Dà Cài Xì)** are the country's most famous regional cooking styles, each with unique ingredients and cooking techniques.

1. Sichuan Cuisine (川菜, Chuān Cài) – *Spicy, Bold, and Numbing* 🌶️

✔ Signature flavors: **Mala (**麻辣**)** – a combination of numbing Sichuan peppercorns and fiery chili peppers.

✔ Famous dishes: **Kung Pao Chicken (**宫保鸡丁**), Mapo Tofu (**麻婆豆腐**), Sichuan Hotpot (**四川火锅**).

✔ Where to try: **Chengdu** – the official UNESCO City of Gastronomy!

2. Cantonese Cuisine (粤菜, Yuè Cài) – *Delicate, Fresh, and Dim Sum Heaven* ⁄⁄

✔ Signature flavors: **Light, natural, and umami-rich**, often using steaming and roasting.
   ✔ Famous dishes: **Dim Sum (**点心**), Roast Goose (**烧鹅**), Wonton Noodles (**云吞面**).**
   ✔ Where to try: **Guangzhou & Hong Kong**, the heart of Cantonese cuisine.

3. Shandong Cuisine (鲁菜, Lǔ Cài) – *Savory, Seafood-Rich, and Northern Elegance* 🦀

✔ Signature flavors: **Umami-packed broths, seafood, and crisp frying techniques**.
   ✔ Famous dishes: **Sweet & Sour Carp (**糖醋鲤鱼**), Dezhou Braised Chicken (**德州扒鸡**).**
   ✔ Where to try: **Jinan & Qingdao**, famous for fresh seafood and rich flavors.

4. Jiangsu Cuisine (苏菜, Sū Cài) – *Refined, Sweet & Savory, and Elegant* 🍲

✔ Signature flavors: **Balanced, mild sweetness, and meticulous knife skills**.
   ✔ Famous dishes: **Lion's Head Meatballs (**狮子头**), Sweet & Sour Mandarin Fish (**松鼠桂鱼**).**
   ✔ Where to try: **Nanjing, Suzhou, and Yangzhou.**

5. Zhejiang Cuisine (浙菜, Zhè Cài) – *Light, Fresh, and Coastal-Inspired* 🦞

✔ Signature flavors: **Fresh seafood, mild seasonings, and a focus on natural taste.**
✔ Famous dishes: **West Lake Vinegar Fish** (西湖醋鱼), **Dongpo Pork** (东坡肉).
✔ Where to try: **Hangzhou, Ningbo, and Shaoxing.**

6. Hunan Cuisine (湘菜, Xiāng Cài) – *Spicy, Smoky, and Flavor-Packed* 🔥

✔ Signature flavors: **Bold chili heat, preserved ingredients, and deep frying.**
✔ Famous dishes: **Chairman Mao's Red Braised Pork** (毛氏红烧肉), **Spicy Steamed Fish Head** (剁椒鱼头).
✔ Where to try: **Changsha, the heart of fiery Hunan flavors.**

7. Fujian Cuisine (闽菜, Mǐn Cài) – *Umami, Brothy, and Seafood-Focused* 🍜

✔ Signature flavors: **Savory broths, fresh seafood, and light herbal infusions.**
✔ Famous dishes: **Buddha Jumps Over the Wall** (佛跳墙), **Drunken Ribs** (醉排骨).
✔ Where to try: **Fuzhou, Xiamen, and Quanzhou.**

8. Anhui Cuisine (徽菜, Huī Cài) – *Rustic, Mountainous, and Wild* 🌿

✔ Signature flavors: **Hearty stews, wild herbs, and earthy flavors**.

✔ Famous dishes: **Li Hongzhang Hotchpotch (**李鸿章杂烩**), Steamed Stone Frog (**石蛙蒸**)**.

✔ Where to try: **Huangshan and Hefei**, where the mountain flavors thrive.

Beyond the Big Eight: Other Notable Cuisines

* **Xinjiang Cuisine** – Spiced lamb skewers, hand-pulled noodles, and Central Asian influences.
* **Tibetan Cuisine** – Butter tea, yak-based dishes, and hearty mountain meals.
* **Yunnan Cuisine** – Wild mushrooms, spicy rice noodles, and tropical flavors.

This breakdown ensures you know **exactly where to go for the most authentic dishes in China**, whether you're after a tongue-numbing Sichuan hotpot or a delicate dim sum brunch. 🍜🔥

Street Food & Local Markets

China's street food scene is an **absolute paradise for food lovers**—bold flavors, sizzling woks, and late-night market adventures make it a must-experience for any traveler. Whether you're wandering through the buzzing night markets of Beijing, tasting skewers in Xi'an, or sipping bubble tea in Shanghai, **there's always something delicious waiting for you.**

✴ Must-Try Chinese Street Foods

🥟 Jianbing (煎饼) – The Ultimate Chinese Crepe

* A **crispy, savory pancake** filled with eggs, hoisin sauce, chili, scallions, and sometimes crispy wonton sheets.
* Best found in **Beijing & Tianjin**, but available nationwide as a breakfast staple.

🍢 Chuan'r (串儿) – Xinjiang-Style Grilled Meat Skewers

* Marinated **lamb, chicken, or beef skewers**, grilled over charcoal and seasoned with cumin and chili.
* Best in **Beijing, Xi'an, and anywhere with a strong Muslim food culture.**

🥟 Shengjianbao (生煎包) – Crispy, Juicy Soup Dumplings

* These **pan-fried soup dumplings** are crispy on the bottom and juicy inside, a perfect street snack.
* Best tried in **Shanghai.**

🍜 Lanzhou Hand-Pulled Noodles (兰州拉面)

* A bowl of **chewy, hand-pulled wheat noodles** served in a fragrant beef broth with chili oil.
* Found all over China but **originates from Lanzhou, Gansu Province.**

🌱 Stinky Tofu (臭豆腐) – The Love-It-Or-Hate-It Classic

- Deep-fried fermented tofu with a crispy outside and **strong, pungent aroma.**
- Best in **Changsha, Shanghai, and night markets across China.**

🫘 Roujiamo (肉夹馍) – The "Chinese Hamburger"

- Slow-cooked, **shredded beef or pork stuffed into a crispy flatbread**, a Xi'an specialty.
- Best in **Xi'an's Muslim Quarter.**

🍡 Tanghulu (糖葫芦) – Candied Hawthorn Skewers

- A traditional **sweet street snack** of hawthorn berries dipped in hard sugar glaze.
- Best found in **Beijing, Harbin, and Shanghai.**

🛍️ Best Street Food Markets & Night Markets in China

📍 Beijing – Wangfujing Snack Street & Ghost Street (簋街)

✔ Famous for **scorpions on a stick, jianbing, and lamb skewers.**
✔ Ghost Street (Guijie) is **the go-to spot for spicy crawfish and Sichuan dishes.**

📍 **Shanghai – Yuyuan Bazaar & Wujiang Road Night Market**

✔ Iconic for **Shengjianbao (pan-fried dumplings) & crab soup dumplings**.
   ✔ Try local desserts like **osmanthus cake & sweet rice balls**.

📍 **Xi'an – Muslim Quarter (**回民街**)**

✔ The best place for **Roujiamo, Biang Biang Noodles, and Pomegranate Juice**.
   ✔ A mix of **Middle Eastern & Chinese flavors**, thanks to the Silk Road influence.

📍 **Chengdu – Jinli Ancient Street & Wuhou Temple Market**

✔ The **spicy capital**—must-tries include **Chengdu Hotpot, Sichuan Rabbit Head, and Dan Dan Noodles**.
   ✔ Street performers and historic vibes make it a must-visit.

📍 **Guangzhou – Shangxiajiu Pedestrian Street & Qingping Market**

✔ The best place to try **dim sum, roast goose, and Cantonese desserts**.
   ✔ Qingping Market has **fresh exotic fruits, herbal medicines, and local delicacies**.

📍 **Kunming – Nanqiang Night Market**

✔ The go-to spot for **Yunnan-style barbecue & tropical fruits**.

✔ Don't miss **Crossing-the-Bridge Noodles and Wild Mushroom Hotpot**.

💡 Pro Tips for Enjoying Street Food in China

✔ **Go where the locals go** – If a stall is packed, it's usually a good sign!

✔ **Cashless payment** – Many vendors only accept **WeChat Pay or Alipay**.

✔ **Try everything, but be mindful** – Some street food can be very spicy or oily, so **pace yourself!**

✔ **Hygiene check** – Look for stalls where the food is made fresh, not sitting out too long.

Whether you're a foodie on a mission or just want a quick snack between sightseeing, **China's street food scene is an experience you won't forget!** 🍴🔥

Fine Dining & Michelin-Star Restaurants

China's fine dining scene is a **harmonious blend of heritage and innovation,** offering some of the most exquisite culinary experiences in the world. From **centuries-old imperial recipes** to **avant-garde molecular gastronomy,** the country boasts a selection of

Michelin-starred restaurants and luxury dining spots that showcase the best of Chinese and international cuisine.

🌟 **Michelin-Starred Restaurants in China**

China is home to some of the highest-rated Michelin restaurants, with culinary hubs like **Beijing, Shanghai, Guangzhou, and Hong Kong** leading the way. Here's where you can indulge in **world-class dining experiences**:

📍 **Beijing – Where Imperial Cuisine Meets Innovation**

✔ **King's Joy (京兆尹) – 3 Michelin Stars**

- 📍 **Location:** 2 Wudaoying Hutong, Dongcheng District, Beijing
- ⁄⁄ A temple of **high-end vegetarian cuisine**, blending traditional flavors with modern artistry.
- 🌟 Signature Dish: **Truffle Mushroom Soup & Osmanthus-Infused Tofu**

✔ **Xin Rong Ji (新荣记) – 3 Michelin Stars**

- 📍 **Location:** 2/F, No. 5 Jinrong Street, Xicheng District, Beijing
- ⁄⁄ Specializing in **premium Taizhou seafood**, with delicate, flavorful dishes.
- 🌟 Signature Dish: **Yellow Croaker Fish Soup**

✔ **Family Li Imperial Cuisine (厉家菜) – 1 Michelin Star**

- 📍 **Location:** 11 Yangfang Hutong, Xicheng District, Beijing
- 🍴 A taste of the **Qing Dynasty's imperial feasts**, cooked using recipes passed down through generations.
- 🌸 Signature Dish: **Red-Braised Pork & Bird's Nest Soup**

📍 **Shanghai – The Heart of Contemporary Chinese Cuisine**

✔ **Ultraviolet by Paul Pairet – 3 Michelin Stars**

- 📍 **Secret Location (revealed upon reservation)**
- 🍴 A **multi-sensory dining experience** with only **10 seats per night**, combining light, sound, and scent with extraordinary dishes.
- 🌸 Signature Dish: **Foie Gras Cigarette & Sea Urchin Toast**

✔ **Fu He Hui (福和慧) – 2 Michelin Stars**

- 📍 **Location:** 1037 Yuyuan Road, Changning District, Shanghai
- 🍴 A **vegetarian fine-dining experience** that focuses on seasonal Chinese ingredients.

- ✺ Signature Dish: **Matsutake Mushroom & Chestnut Soup**

✔ T'ang Court (唐阁) – 2 Michelin Stars

- 📍 **Location:** The Langham Hotel, 99 Madang Road, Xintiandi, Shanghai
- ⫻ A Cantonese fine-dining restaurant offering **authentic dim sum and Peking duck.**
- ✺ Signature Dish: **Braised Whole Abalone in Oyster Sauce**

📍 Guangzhou – The Birthplace of Cantonese Fine Dining

✔ Jiang by Chef Fei (江) – 2 Michelin Stars

- 📍 **Location:** Mandarin Oriental, 389 Tianhe Road, Guangzhou
- ⫻ Modern interpretations of **classic Cantonese dishes,** using top-tier ingredients.
- ✺ Signature Dish: **Crispy Roast Suckling Pig & Steamed Crab with Aged Rice Wine**

✔ Song (颂) – 1 Michelin Star

- 📍 **Location:** 3/F, No. 14 Huacheng Avenue, Zhujiang New Town, Guangzhou
- ⫻ A fine-dining experience with a **fusion of Cantonese and Western flavors.**

- ☀ Signature Dish: **Lobster in Champagne Sauce**

📍 Chengdu – Sichuan Cuisine with a Modern Twist

✔ Yu Zhi Lan (玉芝兰) – 1 Michelin Star

- 📍 **Location:** 24 Changfa Street, Qingyang District, Chengdu
- ∥ A boutique dining experience that **redefines Sichuan cuisine** with elegant, delicate dishes.
- ☀ Signature Dish: **Tea-Smoked Duck & Handmade Sichuan Dumplings**

✔ Chen Mapo Tofu (陈麻婆豆腐) – Bib Gourmand

- 📍 **Location:** 197 West Yulong Street, Qingyang District, Chengdu
- ∥ The **legendary birthplace of Mapo Tofu**, serving the dish in its most authentic form.
- ☀ Signature Dish: **Mapo Tofu with Minced Pork & Fermented Black Beans**

🍷 High-End International Dining in China

China's fine dining scene isn't just about **local flavors**—it's also home to some of the best **French, Italian, and Japanese restaurants** in Asia.

✔ **Robuchon au Dôme (Macau) – 3 Michelin Stars**

- One of **Joël Robuchon's finest restaurants**, serving exquisite French cuisine with **panoramic city views**.

✔ **8½ Otto e Mezzo BOMBANA (Shanghai) – 3 Michelin Stars**

- A legendary **Italian fine-dining restaurant**, famous for **truffle-infused dishes**.

✔ **Sushi Saito (Hong Kong) – 3 Michelin Stars**

- Considered one of the **best sushi restaurants outside Japan**, known for its **precise, delicate craftsmanship**.

💡 Pro Tips for Fine Dining in China

✔ **Book in advance** – Michelin-starred restaurants fill up quickly, so **reservations are a must**.

✔ **Dress appropriately** – Some high-end venues have a **smart casual or formal dress code**.

✔ **Be adventurous** – Many restaurants **offer tasting menus**, allowing you to try a variety of unique dishes.

✔ **Check for WeChat Pay/Alipay** – Some fine-dining spots may not accept international credit cards.

Whether you're indulging in **Peking duck at an imperial banquet**, savoring **Sichuan spice in a refined setting**, or experiencing **cutting-edge molecular gastronomy**, China's fine-dining landscape is a journey **worth every bite!** 🍽️✨

How to Eat Like a Local

Eating like a local in China isn't just about **what you eat**—it's about **where, how, and with whom** you eat. From hole-in-the-wall eateries to bustling night markets and family-style banquets, food culture in China is deeply **communal, diverse, and steeped in tradition**. If you want to truly experience the country's rich culinary heritage, **ditch the touristy spots and follow the locals.**

🍜 Where the Locals Eat

✔ **Street Food & Night Markets** – The heart of local dining culture. Some of the best food in China comes from street vendors and late-night food stalls.

- 📍 **Wangfujing Snack Street (Beijing)** – Scorpions on a stick, anyone? A mix of adventurous and traditional street foods.
- 📍 **Yongkang Road (Shanghai)** – A vibrant mix of local dumpling stalls and trendy fusion bites.

- 📍 **Jinli Ancient Street (Chengdu)** – A paradise for spicy Sichuan snacks like **Chuan Chuan skewers** and **sweet rice cakes**.

✔ **Mom-and-Pop Restaurants** (小吃店) – Family-run eateries serving **authentic home-style dishes** at unbeatable prices.

- ⚫ **Look for handwritten menus** – These usually indicate a local favorite with fresh, rotating dishes.
- ⫽ **Observe where locals are lining up** – If it's crowded with locals, it's probably delicious!

✔ **Dai Pai Dongs & Food Courts** – Open-air food stalls (especially popular in **Guangdong and Hong Kong**) where locals grab quick, tasty meals.

- 📍 **Temple Street Night Market (Hong Kong)** – Famous for claypot rice, salt & pepper squid, and wok-fried noodles.

✔ **Tea Houses & Dumpling Houses** – Dim sum in **Guangzhou**, dumplings in **Xi'an**, and steamed buns in **Shanghai** are essential experiences.

- 📍 **Lin Heung Tea House (Hong Kong)** – One of the last **old-school dim sum halls** where food is served from pushcarts.

🍖 Essential Local Dining Etiquette

✔ **Sharing is Key** – **Chinese meals are served family-style**, with multiple dishes in the center for sharing. Individual portions are rare.

✔ **Use Chopsticks Correctly** – Never stick chopsticks upright in rice (it resembles funeral incense) or point them at others.

✔ **Bargain at Markets** – In some night markets, bargaining is common—**but not at sit-down restaurants**.

✔ **Slurping & Noise? Normal!** – Slurping noodles is **a sign of appreciation**, not bad manners.

✔ **Toasting Culture** – If drinking **baijiu (strong Chinese liquor)**, wait for someone to toast before sipping. **Saying "Ganbei" (干杯) means drink it all!**

🛡 How to Order Like a Pro

🚫 **Avoid Menus with Pictures Only** – If a restaurant only has an English menu with pictures, it's likely catering to tourists. Ask for the **Chinese menu (菜单, càidān)** for more authentic options.

💡 **Must-Know Ordering Tips:**

- **"Zhège hěn là ma?"** (这个很辣吗?) – "Is this very spicy?"
- **"Wǒ yào yī gè zhè lǐ zuì tèsè de cài"** (我要一个这里最特色的菜) – "I'd like your signature dish."

- **"Bú yào wèijīng"** (不要味精) – "No MSG, please."

⁄⁄ Local Dishes You Can't Miss

✔ **Beijing – Peking Duck** (北京烤鸭) 🦆
✔ **Sichuan – Hot Pot** (火锅) 🌶 & **Mapo Tofu** (麻婆豆腐) 🌶
✔ **Shanghai – Xiaolongbao** (小笼包) **Soup Dumplings** 🥟
✔ **Guangzhou – Dim Sum** (点心) 🥟
✔ **Xi'an – Biang Biang Noodles** (油泼扯面) 🍜
✔ **Yunnan – Crossing the Bridge Noodles** (过桥米线) 🍲

💡 Pro Tips for Eating Like a Local

✔ **Eat at Off-Peak Hours** – Avoid the lunch and dinner rush (12-2 PM & 6-8 PM) for the best service and freshest food.

✔ **Cash & Mobile Payment Only** – Some small eateries don't accept foreign cards, so use **WeChat Pay or Alipay**.

✔ **Don't Expect Customization** – Unlike Western restaurants, most Chinese eateries don't do substitutions or custom orders.

✔ **Go Beyond the Cities** – Rural areas have **hidden culinary treasures** that are more authentic than big city dining.

When in China, **eat as the locals do**—and that means being adventurous, trying new dishes, and embracing the

chaotic, delicious, and unforgettable experience of Chinese food culture! 🍜🥢

Chapter 7: Shopping, Souvenirs & Nightlife

China is a **shopper's paradise**, offering everything from high-end luxury brands to bustling markets filled with unique souvenirs. Whether you're hunting for traditional handicrafts, high-tech gadgets, or trendy fashion, the country's diverse shopping scene has something for everyone. But shopping isn't the only way to experience China's vibrant energy—**when the sun sets, the nightlife comes alive**, with rooftop bars, neon-lit night markets, and thrilling entertainment options across the country.

This chapter will guide you through **the best shopping spots, must-buy souvenirs, and the dynamic nightlife scene**, ensuring you make the most of your evenings in China.

🛍 What You'll Discover in This Chapter:

✔ **Best Shopping Streets & Markets** – From Beijing's Silk Market to Shanghai's Nanjing Road.
　✔ **Authentic Souvenirs to Bring Home** – Tea, silk, ceramics, jade, and more.
　✔ **How to Bargain Like a Local** – Master the art of negotiation in China's markets.
　✔ **China's Thriving Nightlife Scene** – The best bars,

clubs, live music venues, and night markets.

✔ **Traditional vs. Modern Nightlife** – From tea houses and opera performances to high-energy clubs and karaoke bars.

Whether you're shopping for treasures or looking for an unforgettable night out, this chapter will ensure you experience the **best of China after dark!** 🌙

Best Shopping Markets & Malls

China offers an **incredible mix of traditional markets and ultra-modern malls**, making it a dream destination for shoppers. Whether you're searching for handcrafted souvenirs, luxury fashion, or cutting-edge technology, **China has it all**. Here's a breakdown of some of the best places to shop across the country:

🛒 Top Traditional Markets

✔ **Silk Market (秀水街), Beijing**
📍 **Address:** 8 Xiushui East Street, Chaoyang District, Beijing
   ◆ Famous for high-quality **silk, clothing, accessories, and souvenirs**. Bargaining is a must!

✔ **Yuyuan Bazaar (豫园市场), Shanghai**
📍 **Address:** 218 Anren Street, Huangpu District, Shanghai
   ◆ Located near the famous Yu Garden, this market is

great for **handicrafts, jewelry, and traditional Chinese goods**.

✔ **Chengdu Jinli Street (**锦里古街**), Chengdu**
 📍 **Address:** Wuhou District, Chengdu, Sichuan
 ◆ A charming, historical street with stalls selling **Tibetan crafts, Shu embroidery, Sichuan snacks, and unique souvenirs**.

✔ **Panjiayuan Antique Market (**潘家园旧货市场**), Beijing**
 📍 **Address:** 18 Huaweili, Chaoyang District, Beijing
 ◆ China's most famous antique market, ideal for finding **jade, calligraphy, paintings, old coins, and vintage furniture**.

✔ **Luohu Commercial City (**罗湖商业城**), Shenzhen**
 📍 **Address:** 5018 Shennan East Road, Luohu District, Shenzhen
 ◆ A haven for **tailor-made clothing, electronics, handbags, and watches** at bargain prices.

🛍️ Best Modern Malls & Luxury Shopping

✔ **IFC Mall, Shanghai**
 📍 **Address:** 8 Century Avenue, Pudong, Shanghai
 ◆ One of Shanghai's most luxurious malls, featuring brands like **Louis Vuitton, Gucci, and Cartier**.

✔ **Taikoo Li Sanlitun (**三里屯太古里**), Beijing**
📍 **Address:** 19 Sanlitun Road, Chaoyang District, Beijing
◆ A trendy, open-air shopping district with **high-end fashion, concept stores, and stylish cafés.**

✔ **The MixC (**万象城**), Shenzhen**
📍 **Address:** 1881 Bao'an South Road, Luohu District, Shenzhen
◆ A massive shopping center with **international brands, gourmet dining, and even an ice-skating rink.**

✔ **Grandview Mall (**正佳广场**), Guangzhou**
📍 **Address:** 228 Tianhe Road, Tianhe District, Guangzhou
◆ A gigantic mall with **fashion, dining, entertainment, and one of the world's largest indoor aquariums**.

✔ **China World Mall, Beijing**
📍 **Address:** 1 Jianguomen Outer Street, Chaoyang District, Beijing
◆ Home to **designer brands, fine dining, and high-end lifestyle stores**.

📍 Shopping Tips for China

✔ **Always bargain at markets** – Prices are often inflated for tourists, so negotiate with confidence!
✔ **Use cash or mobile payments** – Many stores prefer **WeChat Pay or Alipay** over credit cards.
✔ **Check for authenticity** – Be cautious when buying

jade, silk, and antiques to avoid fakes.
✔ **Plan your tax refunds** – Some malls offer tax rebates for tourists on luxury purchases.

Whether you're hunting for a bargain or indulging in designer brands, shopping in China is an adventure in itself! 🛍️

Bargaining Like a Pro

Bargaining is a **fundamental skill** when shopping at markets, street stalls, and smaller shops in China. Unlike fixed-price malls, many places expect you to haggle—it's part of the culture! Mastering the **art of negotiation** will not only save you money but also make the shopping experience more fun and engaging.

🛒 Where Can You Bargain?

✔ **Street markets & night markets** – Souvenir stands, clothing, and accessories.
✔ **Local craft & antique markets** – Items like jade, paintings, and ceramics.
✔ **Electronics & gadget stores** – Particularly in tech hubs like Shenzhen.
✔ **Tailor shops & fabric markets** – Custom suits, qipaos, and fabrics.

✔ **Some small independent shops** – Usually outside of tourist-heavy areas.

📌 **Where You CAN'T Bargain:** Department stores, supermarkets, luxury malls, and chain stores.

🛠 How to Bargain Like a Local

✔ 1. Start with a Friendly Attitude ⚫
A smile and a bit of humor can go a long way. Vendors enjoy the bargaining process and are more likely to give a good deal if you're polite and engaging.

✔ 2. Know the Real Price 🏷
Vendors usually **inflate prices**, especially for tourists. A general rule: **aim for 30-50% of the initial price** and work from there.

✔ 3. Act Disinterested ⚫
If you seem too eager, the seller won't lower the price much. Instead, act as if you're considering multiple options or casually browsing.

✔ 4. Offer a Low But Reasonable Price 💰
Start by offering **around 25-30% of the asking price**. The vendor will counter with a higher price, and you'll meet somewhere in the middle.

✔ 5. Be Ready to Walk Away 🚶

One of the best tactics! If the seller won't lower the price, say "Too expensive" (太贵了, tài guì le) and start walking away. Most of the time, they'll call you back with a better deal.

✔ 6. Cash is King 🏦

Although mobile payments (WeChat Pay, Alipay) are common, having cash in smaller denominations makes bargaining easier and gives you an advantage.

✔ 7. Buy More, Pay Less 🛍️

If you're getting multiple items, ask for a **bulk discount**. Many vendors will offer a better deal if you buy in quantity.

✔ 8. Play the "Local Price" Card 📱

Try saying:

🗣️ **"Tài guì le! Wǒ shì xuéshēng"** (太贵了！我是学生) – "Too expensive! I'm a student."

🗣️ **"Wǒ zhīdào zhèlǐ de zhēnzhèng jiàgé"** (我知道这里的真正价格) – "I know the real price here."

✔ 9. The Final Offer Strategy ⚫

If you've reached a standstill, make a **final take-it-or-leave-it offer**. If they refuse, simply thank them and walk away—often, they'll call you back with a lower price.

✔ 10. Have Fun! 🐘

Bargaining is an experience, not just a transaction. Enjoy the back-and-forth, and don't take it too seriously!

💡 Bonus Tip: Use Local Help

If you're struggling, **ask a local friend or hotel staff** about reasonable prices before heading out. They might even bargain on your behalf!

📌 Key Phrase to Remember:
🗣 **"Kěyǐ piányi yīdiǎn ma?"** (可以便宜一点吗?) – "Can you lower the price a little?"

With these **pro bargaining skills**, you'll be walking away with the **best deals** like a true local! 💪🛍

Nightlife & Entertainment

When the sun sets over China, a whole new world awakens. From vibrant rooftop bars to underground clubs and traditional performances, the nightlife here is as diverse as the country itself. Whether you're looking for an evening of fine cocktails in a sleek modern venue or an authentic night at a local karaoke bar, there's something to suit every taste and mood.

Top Nightlife Destinations

- **Sanlitun, Beijing:**
  Known for its international vibe, Sanlitun is packed with trendy bars, bustling clubs, and lively outdoor cafes. It's a great place to mingle with locals and expats alike, enjoying everything from craft beers to innovative cocktails.

- **The Bund, Shanghai:**
  The Bund not only offers iconic views of Shanghai's skyline but also hosts chic rooftop lounges and sophisticated bars. Enjoy a glass of wine or a signature cocktail as you gaze over the neon-lit skyline and the Huangpu River.

- **Lan Kwai Fong, Hong Kong:**
  This internationally renowned district is a hotspot for partygoers, featuring an eclectic mix of pubs, clubs, and international restaurants. It's perfect for a night out that ranges from casual drinks to all-night dance parties.

- **Xintiandi, Shanghai:**
  An elegant fusion of old and new, Xintiandi is famous for its preserved Shikumen architecture, now housing stylish restaurants, cocktail bars, and live music venues. It's ideal for a more relaxed,

upscale evening.

- **Chengdu's Jiujiang Avenue:**
  Known for its laid-back vibe, Chengdu offers a mix of trendy bars and local teahouses that transform into live music venues at night. Here, you can experience everything from indie bands to traditional Sichuan opera performances.

Cultural Entertainment & Traditional Performances

Beyond modern clubs and bars, China offers a variety of cultural entertainment that brings its rich heritage to life:

- **Chinese Opera & Acrobatics:**
  Catch a mesmerizing performance of Peking Opera in Beijing or an acrobatic show in Shanghai. These shows offer a glimpse into traditional Chinese storytelling and skill, often held in theaters or cultural centers.

- **Karaoke (KTV):**
  A favorite among locals, KTV is more than just singing—it's a social event. Rent a private room with friends in cities like Guangzhou or Shenzhen and enjoy the ultimate karaoke experience complete

with snacks and drinks.

- **Night Markets & Street Performances:**
  Explore the lively night markets in cities like Xi'an and Chengdu. Here, the atmosphere is electric with street performers, local food vendors, and spontaneous music—perfect for a relaxed evening stroll or a spontaneous dance session under the stars.

Insider Tips for an Unforgettable Night Out

- **Plan Ahead:**
  Some of the trendiest spots, especially rooftop lounges and high-end clubs, can get crowded. It's a good idea to check online reviews and make reservations if possible.

- **Local Payment Methods:**
  Most venues accept WeChat Pay or Alipay, so make sure your mobile payment apps are set up before you go.

- **Safety First:**
  Use reputable taxi apps like DiDi to get around safely at night, and always keep an eye on your

belongings.

- **Embrace the Local Vibe:**
  Even if you're used to a different nightlife scene, try to step out of your comfort zone. Engage with locals, try regional cocktails, and immerse yourself in the diverse cultural experiences that each city has to offer.

By diving into China's nightlife and entertainment, you'll not only experience the energy of its modern urban culture but also connect with traditions that have evolved over centuries. Whether you're sipping cocktails on a skyscraper rooftop or belting out your favorite tunes in a cozy KTV room, China's after-dark magic is sure to leave a lasting impression.

Chapter 8: Outdoor Adventures & Wellness Travel

China isn't just about bustling cities and ancient temples—it's also a paradise for outdoor enthusiasts and wellness seekers. From the breathtaking peaks of Zhangjiajie to the tranquil waters of Hangzhou's West Lake, China's diverse landscapes offer a perfect blend of adventure and relaxation. Whether you're a thrill-seeker looking to conquer rugged trails or a traveler in search of a peaceful retreat, this chapter will guide you to the best nature escapes and wellness experiences across the country.

What to Expect in This Chapter:

- **Epic Hiking & Trekking Spots:** Discover legendary trails like the Tiger Leaping Gorge and the Great Wall's wild sections for an unforgettable journey through China's landscapes.

- **Scenic Waterways & Cruises:** Explore the beauty of the Li River, the Yangtze Three Gorges, and serene mountain lakes that offer a refreshing escape from urban life.

- **Hot Springs & Traditional Wellness Retreats:** Immerse yourself in the centuries-old Chinese wellness culture with visits to natural hot springs, meditation retreats, and traditional medicine spas.

- **National Parks & Wildlife Reserves:** Encounter rare species like giant pandas in Sichuan or explore the stunning rock formations of Danxia Landform Geopark.

- **Outdoor Sports & Activities:** From skiing in Harbin's ice kingdom to cycling through Yunnan's breathtaking landscapes, China has something for every outdoor lover.

Whether you're seeking an adrenaline rush or a calming escape, this chapter will help you explore the best of China's great outdoors while embracing its deep-rooted wellness traditions.

Best Hiking & Nature Destinations

China's vast and varied terrain offers some of the most stunning hiking and nature experiences in the world. From dramatic mountain peaks to deep river gorges and lush bamboo forests, every region has something unique to offer for outdoor enthusiasts. Whether you're a seasoned trekker or a casual hiker, these destinations provide an unforgettable escape into nature.

1. Zhangjiajie National Forest Park (Hunan Province)

- **Why Go?** The inspiration for the floating mountains in *Avatar*, Zhangjiajie is famous for its towering sandstone pillars, lush forests, and misty valleys.

- **Top Trails:** The Golden Whip Stream Trail offers a scenic, moderate hike, while the Tianmen Mountain

Stairway is a thrilling challenge with panoramic views.

---

2. Tiger Leaping Gorge (Yunnan Province)

- **Why Go?** One of the deepest and most spectacular river gorges in the world, this trail follows the Jinsha River with breathtaking cliffs and waterfalls.

- **Top Trails:** The classic two-day hike along the High Trail offers the best views and a chance to stay in local guesthouses.

---

3. Mount Huangshan (Yellow Mountains, Anhui Province)

- **Why Go?** Known for its dramatic granite peaks, ancient pine trees, and mystical sea of clouds, Huangshan is one of China's most iconic natural landscapes.

- **Top Trails:** The Western Sea Grand Canyon route offers a more secluded and challenging hike, while the Eastern Steps Trail is an easier ascent with cable car access.

---

4. Jiuzhaigou Valley (Sichuan Province)

- **Why Go?** A UNESCO World Heritage Site, Jiuzhaigou is famous for its crystal-clear turquoise lakes, multi-tiered waterfalls, and colorful forests.

- **Top Trails:** While most visitors take the shuttle bus, several walking paths allow you to explore the stunning scenery at a slower pace.

---

5. The Great Wall of China – Wild Sections (Beijing & Hebei Provinces)

- **Why Go?** While the popular sections like Badaling are crowded, the wild, unrestored sections of the Great Wall offer a more authentic and adventurous hiking experience.

- **Top Trails:** Jiankou (steep and rugged for experienced hikers) and Gubeikou (a less crowded alternative with amazing views).

6. Li River & Karst Mountains (Guilin & Yangshuo, Guangxi Province)

- **Why Go?** Famous for its surreal karst peaks and serene river landscapes, this region is perfect for hiking and bamboo rafting.

- **Top Trails:** The hike from Xingping to Yangdi offers breathtaking river views, and Moon Hill in Yangshuo provides a rewarding short climb.

7. Mount Everest Base Camp (Tibet Autonomous Region)

- **Why Go?** The ultimate trek for adventure seekers, the Tibetan side of Everest offers an awe-inspiring view of the world's highest peak.

- **Top Trails:** The trek from Old Tingri to Everest Base Camp takes about four days and passes through remote Tibetan villages and monasteries.

8. Danxia Landform Geopark (Gansu & Guangdong Provinces)

- **Why Go?** Known for its otherworldly red rock formations, this UNESCO-listed site offers unique landscapes unlike anywhere else in China.

- **Top Trails:** The Rainbow Mountains in Zhangye and the red cliffs of Mount Danxia offer easy-to-moderate hikes with jaw-dropping scenery.

---

9. Wulingyuan Scenic Area (Hunan Province)

- **Why Go?** Home to thousands of quartzite sandstone pillars, deep ravines, and stunning caves, this area offers some of China's most spectacular natural scenery.

- **Top Trails:** The Bailong Elevator trail provides easy access to breathtaking viewpoints, while the Yellow Stone Village trail offers a moderate hike with fewer crowds.

---

10. Mount Emei (Sichuan Province)

- **Why Go?** One of China's Four Sacred Buddhist Mountains, Mount Emei is a spiritual and scenic hiking destination known for its ancient monasteries and golden summit views.

- **Top Trails:** The full hike to the Golden Summit is a challenging multi-day trek, but shorter routes are available for those with limited time.

Pro Tips for Hiking in China:

■ **Pack smart** – Bring comfortable hiking shoes, layers for changing weather, and plenty of water.
■ **Plan ahead** – Some national parks require entrance tickets and may have restrictions on independent hiking.
■ **Respect nature** – Stay on designated trails, and avoid littering or disturbing wildlife.
■ **Prepare for altitude** – If hiking in high-altitude areas like Tibet, allow time to acclimatize.

Whether you're exploring misty mountains, deep gorges, or ancient sacred peaks, hiking in China is an adventure that reveals the country's natural wonders like nothing else.

Traditional Chinese Medicine & Wellness Retreats

China has a rich history of wellness practices rooted in Traditional Chinese Medicine (TCM), a system that has been refined over thousands of years. From herbal remedies and acupuncture to tai chi and meditation, TCM emphasizes balance, harmony, and the body's ability to heal itself. For travelers seeking relaxation, rejuvenation, or a deeper understanding of these ancient healing traditions, China offers a wealth of wellness retreats and experiences.

---

1. Understanding Traditional Chinese Medicine (TCM)

TCM is based on the concept of **Qi (life energy)** and the balance of **Yin and Yang** within the body. It includes:

- **Herbal Medicine** – Healing through natural plant-based remedies.

- **Acupuncture** – The use of thin needles to stimulate energy points.

- **Cupping Therapy** – A technique using suction cups to promote circulation.

- **Gua Sha** – A scraping technique to relieve tension and improve circulation.

- **Moxibustion** – The burning of dried mugwort near the skin to enhance healing.

---

2. Top Wellness Retreats & Healing Destinations

🌿 Huangshan TCM & Hot Spring Retreat (Anhui Province)

- Nestled in the scenic Yellow Mountains, this retreat combines TCM therapies with **hot spring bathing**, herbal treatments, and guided meditation.

🏯 The Taoist Wellness Retreat at Wudang Mountains (Hubei Province)

- Wudang is the birthplace of Taoism and **Tai Chi**, offering programs that blend **martial arts, Qigong, and Taoist meditation** for both physical and spiritual well-being.

⬛ Chengdu TCM & Tea Wellness Escape (Sichuan Province)

- Famous for its slow-paced lifestyle, Chengdu offers TCM healing centers, **cupping therapy**, and **herbal tea therapy**, often paired with visits to the city's serene teahouses.

■ Hainan Island Spa & Longevity Retreat (Sanya, Hainan Province)

- Sometimes called the "Hawaii of China," Sanya boasts **luxury spa resorts** that incorporate TCM healing, hydrotherapy, and **ocean therapy** to revitalize the body and mind.

---

3. TCM-Inspired Wellness Activities

■ **Tai Chi & Qigong** – Practicing these slow, controlled movements in parks like **Beijing's Temple of Heaven** or **Shanghai's Fuxing Park** offers a great way to experience the meditative side of Chinese wellness.

■ **Herbal Medicine Consultations** – Visit a **TCM pharmacy** in cities like Beijing, Shanghai, or Chengdu, where experienced herbalists diagnose and prescribe natural remedies based on pulse reading and tongue analysis.

■ **Detox & Fasting Programs** – Many wellness centers offer traditional **TCM detox diets**, incorporating medicinal soups and teas that help balance digestion and promote internal harmony.

■ **Mindfulness & Meditation** – Temples like the **Shaolin Monastery** and **Putuo Mountain Buddhist Retreat** provide immersive meditation retreats for those seeking spiritual healing.

---

4. How to Experience TCM Like a Local

- **Morning Tai Chi Sessions** – Join locals in city parks at sunrise for free tai chi lessons.

- **Traditional Tea Houses** – Experience the healing power of tea at historical spots like **Lao She Teahouse (Beijing)** or **Huxinting Tea House (Shanghai)**.

- **Foot Reflexology & TCM Massages** – A must-try in cities like **Guangzhou, Chengdu, and Hangzhou**, where highly skilled therapists use pressure points to relieve stress and improve circulation.

---

5. Wellness Travel Tips for China

■ **Choose reputable wellness centers** – Look for government-certified TCM clinics to ensure authentic treatments.

■ **Communicate your health needs** – Some treatments may not be suitable for everyone; always discuss concerns with a trained practitioner.

■ **Try a balanced approach** – Combine TCM with China's other wellness offerings, such as **hot springs, tea therapy, and forest bathing** for a full-body rejuvenation experience.

Whether you're looking for **stress relief, better energy flow, or a deeper understanding of TCM**, China offers an incredible array of wellness experiences. From the misty **Wudang Mountains** to the tranquil **teahouses of Chengdu**, exploring Chinese wellness traditions can be both an enlightening and restorative journey.

Eco-Tourism & Sustainable Travel Tips

China's breathtaking landscapes, from the lush rice terraces of **Longji** to the vast grasslands of **Inner Mongolia**, offer endless opportunities for eco-conscious travelers. As China continues to prioritize sustainable tourism, many destinations now focus on environmental preservation, responsible tourism, and cultural appreciation. Whether you're hiking in remote regions, exploring UNESCO-listed nature reserves, or supporting local communities, here's how you can experience China sustainably while leaving a positive impact.

---

1. Top Eco-Tourism Destinations in China

🌱 **Jiuzhaigou National Park (Sichuan Province)** – A UNESCO World Heritage site known for its **turquoise lakes, cascading waterfalls, and snow-capped peaks**. Jiuzhaigou has strict visitor limits to protect its fragile ecosystem.

⛰️ **Zhangjiajie National Forest Park (Hunan Province)** – Famous for its towering sandstone pillars (inspiration for *Avatar*'s floating mountains), Zhangjiajie has eco-friendly boardwalks and shuttle buses to minimize environmental impact.

🐼 **Wolong National Nature Reserve (Sichuan Province)** – A **panda conservation area** dedicated to protecting endangered giant pandas and other rare species in their natural habitat.

🌾 **Yuanyang Rice Terraces (Yunnan Province)** – Ancient terraces cultivated by the **Hani people**, offering stunning scenery and an authentic insight into sustainable farming practices.

⬛ **Kanas Nature Reserve (Xinjiang Province)** – A hidden gem with **pristine lakes, alpine forests, and nomadic**

Kazakh culture, promoting eco-friendly tourism in China's remote northwest.

---

2. How to Travel Sustainably in China

■ **Choose Green Accommodations** – Stay at **eco-lodges, guesthouses, or sustainable hotels** that use renewable energy and minimize waste. Platforms like **Green Hotel China** list eco-certified stays.

■ **Support Local Communities** – Buy handicrafts directly from **ethnic minority villages**, dine at family-run restaurants, and hire **local guides** for an authentic and responsible experience.

■ **Minimize Plastic Waste** – Bring a **reusable water bottle** (many public places have free refill stations), say no to **single-use plastics**, and carry **reusable shopping bags** for markets.

■ **Respect Wildlife & Nature** – Avoid unethical **animal tourism** (like staged panda encounters or elephant rides) and never pick plants or disrupt natural habitats.

■ **Use Eco-Friendly Transport** – Opt for **China's high-speed trains, biking, or public transport** instead of short-haul flights. Cities like **Beijing, Shanghai, and Hangzhou** have excellent metro and bike-sharing networks.

3. Ethical Wildlife & Conservation Travel

🐨 **Chengdu Panda Base & Dujiangyan Panda Valley** – Instead of touristy panda parks, visit **ethical panda conservation centers** where you can learn about rehabilitation and protection efforts.

🐦 **Poyang Lake Wetlands (Jiangxi Province)** - A critical bird migration site, home to **Siberian cranes and rare waterfowl,** offering **eco-friendly boat tours** with minimal disturbance to wildlife.

🐬 **Taozi Bay (Guangdong Province)** – A sustainable dolphin-watching destination where operators follow **strict ethical guidelines** to protect **Chinese white dolphins** in their natural habitat.

🌳 **Shennongjia Forest (Hubei Province)** – A UNESCO-listed biosphere reserve known for its diverse plant species and rare **golden snub-nosed monkeys,** promoting responsible wildlife tourism.

4. Best Eco-Friendly Activities in China

🌿 **Hiking & Nature Walks** – Explore sustainable trekking routes like **Tiger Leaping Gorge (Yunnan)** or the **Hua**

Shan Plank Walk (Shaanxi), ensuring you follow "leave no trace" principles.

🚵 **Cycling in the Countryside** – Rent a bike in **Yangshuo, Hangzhou, or Xishuangbanna** for a scenic ride through rice fields, karst mountains, and tea plantations.

🌾 **Organic Farm Visits** – Experience sustainable farming at **Hani rice terraces, Dali's organic farms, or Guilin's tea plantations**, learning about traditional **eco-friendly agriculture**.

⬛ **Eco-Village Stays** – Immerse yourself in **Tibetan homestays in Gansu, Dong villages in Guizhou**, or **Kazakh yurts in Xinjiang**, supporting local sustainability efforts.

🚣 **Eco-Friendly River Cruises** – Instead of diesel-powered cruises, opt for **traditional bamboo rafting on the Li River (Guilin)** or **solar-powered boat rides on West Lake (Hangzhou)**.

---

5. Sustainable Travel Etiquette in China

⬛ **Respect local cultures** – Dress modestly in **ethnic minority villages** and participate in traditions with an open mind.
⬛ **Say no to wildlife souvenirs** – Avoid buying products made from ivory, tortoiseshell, or rare animal skins.

■ **Follow eco-park rules** – Stick to designated paths in nature reserves, don't feed wild animals, and avoid using loud music or drones that disturb wildlife.

■ **Reduce food waste** – Order only what you can eat, as food waste is a major issue in many Chinese cities.

Eco-tourism in China is rapidly growing, offering incredible opportunities to experience **nature, wildlife, and cultural heritage** in a responsible way. By making small, mindful choices, you can explore China sustainably while helping to preserve its natural beauty for future generations. ●♻

Chapter 9: Photography & Social Media Travel in China

China is a paradise for photographers, offering a mix of **ancient history, futuristic skylines, breathtaking landscapes, and vibrant street scenes**. Whether you're capturing the towering **Great Wall at sunrise**, the neon-lit streets of **Shanghai**, or the misty karst mountains of **Guilin**, China provides endless opportunities for stunning photography.

At the same time, social media plays a massive role in modern travel, helping you share your experiences, connect with other travelers, and even navigate the country more easily. However, **China's internet landscape**

is unique, with platforms like **WeChat, Xiaohongshu, and Weibo** dominating the scene. This chapter will guide you through the best **photo spots, social media tips, and essential apps** to enhance your travel experience.

Key Topics Covered:

📕 **Best Photography Spots in China** – From the **Forbidden City in Beijing** to the **Zhangjiajie Avatar Mountains**, discover the country's most photogenic locations.

📷 **Photography Tips & Etiquette** – How to capture stunning shots while being respectful of local culture and laws.

📱 **Navigating China's Social Media** – An introduction to **WeChat, Xiaohongshu, Douyin (China's TikTok), and Weibo** for travel sharing.

⚫ **How to Stay Connected** – The best **VPNs, SIM cards, and Wi-Fi hotspots** to access global social media platforms.

🚀 **Trending Travel Hashtags & Influencer Insights** – Boost your reach on platforms like **Instagram, Xiaohongshu, and WeChat Moments** with top travel hashtags and engagement tips.

Whether you're a casual traveler looking for the perfect snapshot or a content creator aiming to build an audience, this chapter will equip you with everything you need to document your China adventure like a pro!

Most Instagrammable Spots

China is packed with jaw-dropping locations that are perfect for capturing envy-worthy Instagram shots. From **ancient wonders** to **modern marvels**, here are some of the most photogenic destinations across the country:

🏯 Iconic Landmarks & Historical Wonders

📍 **The Great Wall of China (Beijing)** – Best at **Mutianyu or Jinshanling** for fewer crowds and breathtaking sunrise views.

📍 **The Forbidden City (Beijing)** – Capture its striking **red walls, golden rooftops, and intricate courtyards**.

📍 **Terracotta Army (Xi'an)** – A surreal shot of **thousands of ancient warriors standing in formation**.

📍 **Potala Palace (Lhasa, Tibet)** – The majestic, sky-high **palace of the Dalai Lama** against a backdrop of blue skies.

🏙 Urban Skylines & Futuristic Architecture

📍 **The Bund (Shanghai)** – The **best skyline view** of Shanghai's futuristic skyscrapers, especially at night.

📍 **Canton Tower (Guangzhou)** – A colorful, twisting tower offering **panoramic city views**.

📍 **Chongqing's Hongya Cave** – A glowing **cyberpunk cityscape** at night, straight out of a sci-fi movie.

🌿 Natural Wonders & Scenic Landscapes

📍 **Zhangjiajie National Forest Park (Hunan)** – The **"Avatar Mountains"**, misty pillars that inspired the floating Hallelujah Mountains in *Avatar*.

📍 **Guilin & Yangshuo (Guangxi)** – Capture **karst mountains, bamboo rafting on the Li River, and dreamy sunrises**.

📍 **Rainbow Mountains (Zhangye Danxia, Gansu)** – Stunning, surreal **multi-colored rock formations** that look painted.

📍 **Huangshan (Yellow Mountain, Anhui)** – A legendary spot with **floating sea clouds, twisted pine trees, and epic sunrises**.

🐘 **Cultural & Hidden Gems**

📍 **Pingyao Ancient City (Shanxi)** – One of China's best-preserved ancient towns, featuring **red lanterns and Ming-era architecture**.

📍 **Fujian Tulou (Fujian Province)** – Unique **circular Hakka houses** built centuries ago, looking like real-life UFOs.

📍 **Jiufen (Taiwan)** – The hillside **lantern-lit town** said to have inspired *Spirited Away*.

📍 **Dongchuan Red Land (Yunnan)** – A lesser-known, mind-blowing landscape of **fiery red, orange, and green fields**.

These spots will make your Instagram feed **stand out**, whether you love dramatic landscapes, historical sites, or dazzling cityscapes! 📷✨

Photography Tips for Capturing China's Landscapes

China's landscapes range from **towering mountains** and **misty rivers** to **ancient architecture** and **futuristic skylines**. To make the most of your shots, follow these expert photography tips:

1 Plan for the Golden Hour

- The best lighting is **early morning (sunrise)** and **late afternoon (sunset)** for warm tones and soft shadows.

- Example: **Capture the Li River in Guilin** at dawn for dreamy mist over the karst mountains.

2 Use a Wide-Angle Lens for Vast Landscapes

- A **16-35mm lens** works great for **expansive mountain ranges, rice terraces, and city skylines**.

- Example: **Zhangjiajie's Avatar Mountains** look more dramatic with a wide frame capturing the floating peaks.

3 Experiment with Leading Lines

- Use **roads, bridges, and river curves** to guide the viewer's eye into the photo.

- Example: The **Great Wall of China's winding path** makes for a powerful leading line shot.

4 Play with Reflections

- Capture **mirrored landscapes** in lakes, rivers, and wet streets after rain.

- Example: The **West Lake in Hangzhou** reflects pagodas and trees beautifully at sunrise.

5 Adjust for China's Dramatic Weather

- **Misty mornings** in Huangshan? Boost contrast to highlight the **mystical mountain peaks**.

- **Bright summer days in Zhangye's Rainbow Mountains?** Use a **polarizing filter** to cut glare and deepen colors.

6 Capture the Scale of Nature

- Place a person in the frame to show how vast the landscape is.

- Example: A **tiny hiker standing on a Huangshan peak** makes the mountains look even grander.

7 Night Photography Tips for Cityscapes

- Use a **tripod** for stable long-exposure shots of Shanghai's **neon skyline**.

- Lower ISO and use a **10-20 second shutter speed** to get crisp city lights.

8 Shoot from Unique Perspectives

- **Drones** work great for **rice terraces, winding rivers, and old towns**.

- Try **low-angle shots** to make **pagodas, mountains, or temples** appear more grand.

9 Adjust for Air Quality & Foggy Conditions

- China can have **hazy days**, especially in big cities. Use:
    - **UV filters** to reduce haze
    - **Dehaze tool in editing** to bring back details
    - **Black & white mode** for moody atmospheric shots

■ Mastering Post-Processing

- Enhance colors in **Zhangye's Rainbow Mountains** without making them look fake.

- Use Lightroom to **boost contrast, sharpness, and clarity** in misty mountain shots.

With these tips, you'll capture **breathtaking landscapes** that truly showcase China's beauty! ●■✦

Understanding Local Restrictions on Social Media Use

When traveling in China, you'll quickly notice that many popular **Western social media platforms and websites**—such as **Facebook, Instagram, WhatsApp, Twitter, and YouTube**—are **blocked** due to the country's strict internet regulations, commonly referred to as the **Great Firewall of China.**

But don't worry—there are ways to stay connected while respecting local laws. Here's what you need to know:

1 What Social Media Is Blocked in China?

The following platforms are **restricted** in mainland China:
- 🚫 **Facebook**
- 🚫 **Instagram**

🚫 **Twitter/X**
🚫 **YouTube**
🚫 **WhatsApp**
🚫 **Google services (Gmail, Maps, Drive, etc.)**

2 What Social Media Platforms Are Popular in China?

Instead of Western apps, China has its own ecosystem of social media and messaging apps:

⬛ **WeChat** (微信, **Wēixìn**) – The ultimate app for messaging, payments, and social media.

⬛ **Weibo** (微博, **Wēibó**) – A microblogging platform, similar to Twitter.

⬛ **Xiaohongshu** (小红书, **"Little Red Book"**) – A mix of Instagram, Pinterest, and e-commerce.

⬛ **Douyin** (抖音, **China's TikTok**) – The original version of TikTok, but different from the international version.

⬛ **Bilibili** (哔哩哔哩, **Bìlībìlī**) – A video-sharing platform like YouTube.

⬛ **Baidu Tieba** (百度贴吧, **Bǎidù Tiēbā**) – A discussion forum similar to Reddit.

3 Can You Access Blocked Sites in China?

To use **Google, Instagram, or WhatsApp**, travelers often rely on a **VPN (Virtual Private Network)**. However, China actively **blocks many VPN services**, so:

✔ **Download and install a VPN before arriving**—some good ones include **ExpressVPN, NordVPN, and Surfshark**.

✔ Keep in mind that **not all VPNs work all the time**, as China updates its firewall restrictions regularly.

✔ Be aware that **VPN use is a gray area**—while foreigners are rarely targeted, it's important to use discretion.

④ What About Messaging & Staying in Touch?

Since **WhatsApp and Facebook Messenger are blocked**, use:
▌ **WeChat** – The most reliable way to chat, make calls, and even translate text.
▌ **Skype** – Works in China without a VPN, but video quality may vary.
▌ **Signal or Telegram** – Sometimes work, but require a VPN.

⑤ Posting Content from China: What to Know

✔ If you're using a VPN, you can still post on Instagram, Facebook, and YouTube.
✔ Alternatively, use **Xiaohongshu or WeChat Moments** to share your China experiences.
✔ Avoid discussing **sensitive political topics** online, as internet censorship is strictly enforced.

By understanding China's social media landscape, you can **stay connected while respecting local regulations**—ensuring a smooth and hassle-free travel experience! ●●

Chapter 10: Practical Travel & Safety Tips

Traveling in China is an exciting adventure, but being well-prepared is key to ensuring a **smooth, safe, and stress-free experience**. This chapter covers essential **travel hacks, safety precautions, health tips, and emergency contacts** to help you navigate China with confidence.

What You'll Learn in This Chapter:

■ **Staying Safe in Crowded Areas** – How to avoid pickpockets and scams in tourist hotspots.

■ **Health & Medical Tips** – Must-know vaccination info, air quality considerations, and where to find medical help.

■ **Emergency Contacts & Numbers** – Who to call if you need help, from police to embassy contacts.

■ **Common Travel Scams & How to Avoid Them** – Recognizing taxi scams, fake tour guides, and overcharging schemes.

■ **Travel Insurance & Why You Need It** – Protecting yourself against trip cancellations, medical emergencies, and lost belongings.

By the end of this chapter, you'll be **fully equipped** with all the essential safety and practical travel tips, ensuring that your journey through China is as **secure and enjoyable** as possible! ✈🏳

Common Scams & How to Avoid Them

China is generally a **safe** country for travelers, but like any major tourist destination, there are **scams** designed to take advantage of unsuspecting visitors. Knowing **what to watch out for** will help you **avoid unnecessary trouble and enjoy your trip stress-free**. Here are some of the most common scams and how to **outsmart them**:

---

1 The Tea House Scam 🍵

How It Works:

A friendly local (often a young woman or student) approaches you, eager to practice their English. They invite you to a traditional tea house for a "cultural experience." After a nice tea session, the bill comes—and it's **outrageously high** (sometimes over ¥1,000+). The scammer may disappear before the check arrives, leaving you stuck with the bill.

■ How to Avoid It:

- Politely decline random invitations from strangers.

- If you want a tea experience, go to a well-known tea house with clear prices.

2 Fake Tour Guides & Attraction Ticket Scams

How It Works:

Outside major landmarks, you may be approached by a "tour guide" offering **discounted** tickets or an "exclusive tour." After paying, you either get a **fake ticket**, an **overpriced basic tour**, or are simply left with nothing.

How to Avoid It:

- Buy tickets **only from official counters or reputable online platforms**.

- If hiring a guide, book through **trusted travel agencies** or hotel recommendations.

3 Taxi & Tuk-Tuk Overcharging

How It Works:

Some **taxi drivers** refuse to use the meter and charge **inflated prices**. Others might **drive you in circles** to increase the fare. In some cases, they may even **swap your cash for counterfeit bills** when giving change.

■ How to Avoid It:

- **Only take licensed taxis** (look for an official logo and driver ID).

- **Insist on the meter** or use ride-hailing apps like **Didi** (滴滴出行) instead.

- **Count your money** carefully when paying and avoid handing over large bills unnecessarily.

---

④ The Art Student Scam 🐾

How It Works:

A "student" or "artist" invites you to an art exhibit or workshop, showcasing their "unique Chinese paintings." Once inside, they pressure you into **buying expensive artwork**, often at **inflated prices**.

■ How to Avoid It:

- Be skeptical of random invitations.

- If you want to buy art, visit **legitimate galleries or art markets**.

5 Counterfeit Money & Shortchange Scams

How It Works:

Some **street vendors, taxi drivers, or small shopkeepers** may give you **fake currency** as change or **claim your bill is fake**, forcing you to pay again.

 How to Avoid It:

- Learn how to recognize **real Chinese yuan (RMB)**—feel the texture and check security features.

- **Pay with small bills** and avoid giving large notes for minor purchases.

- Use digital payment apps like **WeChat Pay** or **Alipay** where possible.

---

6 The Friendly "Bar Scam"

How It Works:

A group of locals (often attractive women) invite you to a bar for drinks. After a fun night, you receive a **ridiculously**

high bill, sometimes in the thousands. If you refuse to pay, **bouncers** may get involved.

■ How to Avoid It:

- Stick to **well-known bars and restaurants**.

- Be cautious of **overly friendly strangers** inviting you to expensive-looking venues.

---

7 Fake Monk Blessings & Begging Scams 🏯

How It Works:

A "monk" offers you a **bracelet or blessing**, then demands **money**—sometimes aggressively. In reality, they are **not real monks** but scammers preying on tourists.

■ How to Avoid It:

- Real monks **never** ask for money in public places.

- Politely refuse and walk away.

Final Travel Tips to Stay Scam-Free 🛡️

✔ **Be skeptical of random invitations** from strangers.
✔ **Use official sources** for tickets, taxis, and tour guides.
✔ **Double-check money and bills** when making transactions.
✔ **Stick to trusted hotels, restaurants, and shops**.
✔ **Trust your gut**—if something feels off, walk away.

By staying **aware and informed**, you'll **avoid scams and fully enjoy** your journey through China! ▪✈

Food Safety & Staying Healthy While Traveling

China's **culinary scene** is an adventure in itself, with everything from sizzling street food to **world-class fine dining**. But while indulging in these flavors, **staying healthy** should be a priority. Here's how to enjoy China's diverse cuisine **without unwanted stomach troubles**.

1️⃣ Tap Water vs. Bottled Water ▪

- **Do NOT drink tap water** in China unless it's **boiled** or **filtered**. Tap water is not safe for drinking due to potential contamination.

- Stick to **bottled, filtered, or boiled water**—easily available at stores, hotels, and restaurants.

- Avoid **ice cubes** unless you're certain they're made from purified water.

---

2 Choosing Safe & Hygienic Restaurants

- **Look for high customer turnover**—if a place is **busy with locals**, it's usually a sign of fresh food.

- Opt for **restaurants with visible hygiene ratings** (China uses an **A, B, C rating system**, with A being the best).

- **Hotel buffets and high-end restaurants** generally have strict hygiene standards.

---

3 Eating Street Food Safely

China's **street food culture** is legendary, but be cautious!

✔ **Go where the locals eat**—a crowd means fresh ingredients.

✔ **Watch how the food is prepared**—choose vendors who cook food fresh in front of you.

✔ **Avoid raw or undercooked meat and seafood** from street stalls.

✔ **Stick to vegetarian options** if you're unsure about meat quality.

---

4 Preventing Traveler's Stomach ●

- Carry **activated charcoal tablets or probiotics** to aid digestion.

- Wash your hands often or use **hand sanitizer** before meals.

- If you have a sensitive stomach, avoid **excessively oily, spicy, or exotic dishes** at first.

- Stick to **fruits that can be peeled** (bananas, oranges) to reduce contamination risks.

---

5 Navigating Food Allergies & Dietary Restrictions |●|

- Learn essential Mandarin phrases for allergies:

  - **I am allergic to peanuts.** → *Wǒ duì huāshēng guòmǐn* (我对花生过敏).

- **No MSG, please.** → *Qǐng bùyào fàng wèijīng* (请不要放味精).

- **I am vegetarian.** → *Wǒ chī sùshí* (我吃素食).

- Many restaurants **use soy sauce that contains gluten**—if you're gluten-sensitive, ask for alternatives.

---

6 Handling Altitude Sickness & Pollution 🧍

- If visiting high-altitude areas like **Tibet or Yunnan**, take it slow to **acclimate** and drink plenty of fluids.

- In cities with **high air pollution (Beijing, Shanghai),** check air quality apps and wear a **mask** on bad days.

---

7 Travel Health Kit Must-Haves 🎒

Pack these essentials for a worry-free food experience:

■ **Antidiarrheal medicine** (like Imodium)
■ **Electrolyte packets** for hydration
■ **Hand sanitizer & disinfectant wipes**

Motion sickness pills (for bumpy roads or boat rides)
Allergy medication (for unexpected reactions)

8 Where to Get Medical Help

- Major cities like **Beijing, Shanghai, Guangzhou** have **international hospitals** with English-speaking staff.

- **Pharmacies** (药店, **Yàodiàn**) are widely available—show symptoms via a translation app if needed.

- **Chinese medicine shops** also offer herbal remedies, but consult a professional before trying new treatments.

Final Tip: Enjoy, But Be Cautious!

Eating in China should be an **exciting and delicious** experience. By following these **food safety tips**, you can **savor every meal without regrets!**

Solo vs. Group Travel Considerations

When planning your **China adventure**, one of the first big decisions is whether to **travel solo or in a group**. Both options offer unique experiences, and the best choice depends on **your preferences, budget, and travel style**. Here's a breakdown to help you decide:

---

1 Solo Travel in China: Freedom & Flexibility

Pros:
✔ **Full control over itinerary** – No need to compromise on where to go or what to do.

✔ **Deeper cultural immersion** – More chances to interact with locals and experience China at your own pace.

✔ **More budget-friendly** – Choose where to splurge and where to save.

✔ **Peaceful & personal experience** – Ideal for independent travelers who enjoy self-exploration.

Challenges:
✘ **Language barrier** – Many locals don't speak English, making communication tricky. Essential Mandarin phrases & translation apps will help.

✘ **Navigation difficulties** – Public transport signage may not always be in English. Using **Baidu Maps** or **WeChat**

Maps (since Google Maps is blocked) is a must.

✘ **Loneliness & safety concerns** – While China is generally safe, being alone means taking extra precautions, especially at night.

● **Best for:** Experienced travelers, adventure seekers, photographers, and those who love spontaneity.

---

② Group Travel in China: Convenience & Social Experience 👥

🔲 **Pros:**
✔ **Less planning hassle** – Tour groups handle visas, accommodations, transport, and attraction bookings.
✔ **Easier communication** – Guides usually speak English and handle interactions with locals.
✔ **Safer experience** – Having travel companions reduces risks and offers support in emergencies.
✔ **Great for first-time visitors** – A structured itinerary ensures you don't miss top attractions.

🔔 **Challenges:**
✘ **Limited flexibility** – Set schedules mean less time for personal exploration.
✘ **Higher cost** – Organized tours often come at a premium.
✘ **Crowded experiences** – You may not get as much time at attractions due to group time constraints.

● **Best for:** First-time travelers, families, history buffs, and those who prefer structured trips.

---

3 The Best of Both Worlds: Small Group or Semi-Guided Tours ▪

For those who want a **mix of freedom and guidance**, small-group tours or **customizable private tours** offer the best of both worlds. You get:

✔ A **local expert** to navigate logistics.
✔ A **flexible itinerary** with free time for self-exploration.
✔ **Social opportunities** without feeling restricted.

🚀 **Pro Tip:** Many cities offer **day tours** to famous sights like the **Great Wall, Terracotta Army, or Guilin's rice terraces**, allowing you to enjoy structure while keeping the rest of your trip independent.

Final Verdict: Which is Right for You? ●

◆ **Go solo if you:** Love flexibility, want an immersive experience, and are comfortable navigating challenges.

◆ **Go with a group if you:** Prefer convenience, want to

meet like-minded travelers, and enjoy structured experiences.

* **Mix both if you:** Want guided assistance for major sights but free days to explore on your own.

No matter how you travel, China's **history, culture, and landscapes** promise an unforgettable journey! ▰✦

Emergency Contacts & Resources for Travelers

When traveling in China, knowing the right emergency contacts and resources can make all the difference in unexpected situations. While China is generally a safe country, it's always best to be prepared. Here's a list of essential emergency numbers, important apps, and useful travel resources to keep on hand.

---

1 Emergency Phone Numbers in China 📞

Unlike in some countries where 911 is a universal emergency number, China has **separate numbers for different types of emergencies**:

* 🚔 **Police: 110** (for crimes, theft, or safety concerns)

- 🚑 **Ambulance: 120** (for medical emergencies)

- 🔥 **Fire Department: 119** (for fires or rescue situations)

- 🚗 **Traffic Accidents: 122** (to report road accidents)

- ⚫ **Foreign Affairs Police: +86-10-5991-4011** (for foreigner-specific assistance)

- ⬛ **Visa & Immigration Issues: +86-10-12367** (24/7 support for visa-related queries)

📌 **Pro Tip:** These emergency lines may not always have English-speaking operators. If in doubt, contact your **hotel concierge** or use translation apps like **Pleco** or **Google Translate** to communicate.

---

2 **Must-Have Apps for Emergency Assistance** ➡️

- ◆ **WeChat (微信)** – Essential for communication, payments, and contacting embassies or local help.
- ◆ **Baidu Maps (百度地图)** – The best alternative to Google Maps, as Google services are blocked in China.
- ◆ **Pleco** – A powerful offline Mandarin-English dictionary

for quick translations.

* **ExpressVPN** – A reliable VPN if you need access to blocked websites (Google, WhatsApp, Facebook, etc.).
* **China Train Booking App** – For booking and managing train tickets efficiently.
* **DiDi (**滴滴**)** – The equivalent of Uber, useful for safe and reliable transport.

---

3 **Foreign Embassies & Consulates**

If you **lose your passport**, need legal assistance, or face a **serious issue**, your **embassy or consulate** is the best place to turn. Below are the embassy contacts for some major countries in **Beijing** (China's capital).

- **U.S. Embassy:** +86-10-8531-4000

- **British Embassy:** +86-10-5192-4000

- **Australian Embassy:** +86-10-5140-4111

- **Canadian Embassy:** +86-10-5139-4000

- **EU Delegation:** +86-10-8454-8000

📍 **Pro Tip:** If you're in a different city, check your embassy's website for the nearest consulate location.

---

4 Medical Assistance & Hospitals

For **serious medical emergencies**, head to **international hospitals** in major cities. These hospitals have **English-speaking doctors** and cater to foreign travelers.

Top International Hospitals in China

📍 **Beijing:** Beijing United Family Hospital (**+86-10-5927-7000**)
📍 **Shanghai:** Parkway Health (**+86-21-6445-5999**)
📍 **Guangzhou:** Clifford Hospital (**+86-20-8471-8123**)
📍 **Chengdu:** Angel Women's & Children's Hospital (**+86-28-8515-9999**)

📍 **Pro Tip:** Always **carry travel insurance** that covers medical emergencies. Many hospitals **require upfront payment**, so having emergency cash or a digital payment method (like **Alipay or WeChat Pay**) is crucial.

---

5 Lost or Stolen Items? What to Do

- **Lost Passport?** 🔔 Contact your **embassy** immediately and file a report at the **nearest police station**.

- **Lost Credit Card?** 💳 Call your bank to **freeze your card** and use a digital wallet like **Alipay** if needed.

- **Lost Phone?** 📱 Use **Find My iPhone** or **Google Find My Device** to track it down.

Final Travel Safety Tips 🛡️

⬛ **Keep digital & paper copies** of your passport, visa, and insurance details.
⬛ **Download offline maps** in case of limited internet access.
⬛ **Learn basic Mandarin phrases** for emergencies.
⬛ **Have a local SIM card** or an eSIM to stay connected.
⬛ **Save emergency numbers in your phone** before your trip.

By staying **prepared and informed**, you can travel **China with confidence and peace of mind!** ●⋆

Printed in Dunstable, United Kingdom

72383548R00097